Cambridge Elements ≡

Elements in Reinventing Capitalism
edited by
Arie Y. Lewin
Duke University
Till Talaulicar
University of Erfurt

REINVENTING CAPITALISM IN THE DIGITAL AGE

Stephen Denning
Senior Contributor, Forbes.com

CAMBRIDGE
UNIVERSITY PRESS

Shaftesbury Road, Cambridge CB2 8EA, United Kingdom

One Liberty Plaza, 20th Floor, New York, NY 10006, USA

477 Williamstown Road, Port Melbourne, VIC 3207, Australia

314–321, 3rd Floor, Plot 3, Splendor Forum, Jasola District Centre, New Delhi – 110025, India

103 Penang Road, #05–06/07, Visioncrest Commercial, Singapore 238467

Cambridge University Press is part of Cambridge University Press & Assessment, a department of the University of Cambridge.

We share the University's mission to contribute to society through the pursuit of education, learning and research at the highest international levels of excellence.

www.cambridge.org
Information on this title: www.cambridge.org/9781009332842

DOI: 10.1017/9781009332880

First published 2022

A catalogue record for this publication is available from the British Library.

ISBN 978-1-009-33284-2 Paperback
ISSN 2634-8950 (online)
ISSN 2634-8942 (print)

Reinventing Capitalism in the Digital Age

Elements in Reinventing Capitalism

DOI: 10.1017/9781009332880
First published online: November 2022

Stephen Denning
Senior Contributor, Forbes.com

Author for correspondence: Stephen Denning, steve@stevedenning.com

Abstract: This Element examines the current crisis of capitalism's legitimacy and concludes that it derives principally from business pursuing an aberration of capitalism known as shareholder capitalism, in which firms sought to maximize shareholder value as reflected in the current share price, at the expense of all other stakeholders and society. Shareholder capitalism began in the 1970s and was renounced by the Business Roundtable in 2019, but continues behind a façade of stakeholder capitalism. Stakeholder capitalism is the most widely cited form of capitalism today, but it is incoherent as a practical guide to action for an entire firm. This Element concludes that a recent evolution of capitalism – customer capitalism – which gives primacy to co-creating value for customers and users, enables firms to master the challenges of the digital age, shower benefits on society, and meet the needs of all the stakeholders.

Keywords: capitalism, shareholder, stakeholder, customer, purpose

ISBNs: 9781009332842 (PB), 9781009332880 (OC)
ISSNs: 2634-8950 (online), 2634-8942 (print)

Contents

1 Introduction

We have been cocksure of many things that were not so.

Oliver Wendell Holmes Jr.[1]

This is an Element in the series, *Reinventing Capitalism*, which features explorations of "the crisis of legitimacy that is facing capitalism today, including the increasing income and wealth gap, the decline of the middle class, threats to employment due to globalization and digitalization, undermined trust in institutions, discrimination against minorities, global poverty, and pollution."

The sections of this Element mainly comprise articles about the past and future of leadership, management, and capitalism that the author published over the past eleven years in Forbes.com, where he is a senior contributor. They reflect both timeless insights as well as the continuing evolution of thinking. The articles have been lightly edited to remove duplication and improve flow.

Three notes on terminology. First, in this Element, capitalism means an economic system based on the private ownership of the means of production and their operation for profit. Although its beginnings were visible much earlier, in this Element, capitalism refers to the modern industrial form of capitalism that began emerging in the late eighteenth century.

Second, the world is so varied that there are exceptions to almost every statement in this Element. To simplify reading, these exceptions are only partly reflected with qualifiers like "mostly" and "often."

Third, while the Element has many global insights, this short volume is mainly focused on capitalism in the United States. That is not meant to diminish the importance of other countries and their viewpoints. A subsequent volume in this series will deepen the analysis of historical and multicountry perspectives.

1.1 Capitalism Is at a Tipping Point

The time is right to reevaluate capitalism for multiple reasons. First, capitalism is widely perceived to be in a crisis and failing large segments of the population.

Second, a vast struggle for the future of human society is under way. Financier Ray Dalio writes:

> "While ages ago, agricultural land and agricultural production were worth the most and that evolved into machines and what they produced being worth the most: digital things that have no apparent physical existence (data and information processing) are now evolving to become worth the most. This is creating a fight over who obtains the data and how they use it to gain wealth and power."[2]

---

[1] "Natural Law," 32 *Harvard Law Review* 40, 41 (1918).

[2] R. Dalio, *Changing World Order: Why Nations Succeed and Fail* (Simon & Schuster, 2021), p. 31.

Capitalism is not just at the tipping point in its predictable life cycle. The fight comes at a time when industrial-era capitalism has put the habitability of the planet at risk.

The choices to be made by countries, companies, and individuals over the next few years could together determine humanity's material future – for better or worse – for the rest of the century, even forever.

Today, countries, companies, and individuals have unique opportunities for broad-based prosperity – and the opposite. The opportunities and risks have many dimensions. This Element is about the management choices needed both to take advantage of the opportunities and to deal with the risks. It also describes broad social and economic ramifications of seemingly narrow management matters.

The choices that decision-makers – and those advising them – now need to make are unlike those they have faced previously, even though most of those dilemmas have occurred several times during capitalism's 250-year history. Thus, in capitalism, societies evolve in slow-moving but predictable life cycles that are longer than the lifespans of individuals. If decision-makers understand what happened before they were born, they may make better decisions. Conversely, if they don't, they may make unnecessary blunders (by contrast, some decisions related to climate change have few precedents). Given the political implications of many of these issues, enhancing fact-based understanding is key to depoliticizing decision-making.

1.2 The Competing Narratives of Capitalism

This Element examines competing narratives that are widely used to explain the situation and to guide decision-making. It reviews the extent to which these narratives are grounded in fact, and which are driven by self-interest, or by misunderstandings of history or of the current situation.

Like *Narrative Economics* (2019), the path-breaking book by Nobel-Prize winning economist, Robert Shiller, this Element examines the dynamic of certain contagious narratives, which themselves can drive major economic and social change. "Ultimately," writes Shiller, "narratives are major vectors of rapid change in culture, in zeitgeist, and in economic behavior."[3]

This Element examines three main narratives: customer capitalism, shareholder capitalism, and stakeholder capitalism, and their roles in the emerging digital age.

[3] R. Shiller, *Narrative Economics: How Stories Go Viral and Drive Major Economic Events* (Princeton University Press, 2019), p. xii. See also: S. Denning, *The Leaders's Guide to Storytelling*, 2nd ed. (Jossey-Bass, 2011).

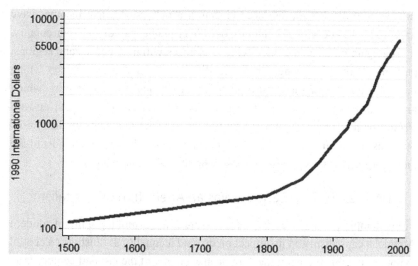

Figure 1 Global average GDP per capita 1500–2000[4]
Source: J.Bradford Delong, "Estimating World GDP, One Million B.C. - Present" (1998)

1.3 The Trajectory of Capitalism

The Element begins with a pervasive – but fallacious – narrative: the meme that everything in the world is getting worse. A comprehensive study presents evidence that questions that narrative and the unwarranted negative pall it casts over current discussions of capitalism.

The study shows that on the key dimensions of material well-being – poverty, literacy, health, freedom, and education – humanity is much better off than it was several centuries ago. This finding implies that we should not rush to judgment from capitalism's current troubles to a conclusion that capitalism itself must be scrapped.

The study suggests that humanity's material condition has significantly improved over the last two centuries, despite wars, plagues, tyrannies, communist policies, corrupt governments, and other disasters. Looking at the 500-year picture in Figure 1, we can see that the turning point in the upward thrust in humanity's material well-being coincided with the spread of capitalism and the industrial revolution in the late eighteenth century.

The fact that most people are materially better off does not alleviate the economic suffering of those individuals, companies and countries that are worse off, or diminish the importance of taking appropriate action to address those issues.

---

[4] This file is licensed under the Creative Commons Attribution-Share Alike 3.0Unported license, https://commons.wikimedia.org/wiki/File:World_GDP_Per_Capita_1500_to_2000,_Log_Scale.png.

It is no consolation to a displaced citizen in a rich country that incomes have improved in less developed countries, or even in another part of their own country.

Aggregate numbers can hide relative changes within countries and regions, particularly relative changes between different income groups. Even where there are no losses, there may be troubling inequalities concerning which group gains. Acute social friction can arise here. Thus, the smooth upward trend shown in Figure 1 gives no hint of the growing inequality in the United States as shown in Figure 2, in which one social class has captured most of the gains for itself at the expense of those who helped create the gains.

1.4 The Last Half Century Was an Aberration of Capitalism

In one simple picture, we can see in Figure 2 the "smoking gun" of modern American capitalism and its impact on income inequality. It illustrates a central hypothesis of this Element: the American economy of the last half century is an aberration of capitalism. Before the 1970s, typical workers' compensation advanced in alignment with the gains in productivity they helped create. After the 1970s, typical workers' compensation stagnated, as the income of other sections of society, particularly executives and shareholders, grew exponentially.[5] We know where the gains went. In the period from 1978 to 2019, CEO compensation has grown 940% while typical worker compensation has risen only 12% during that time.[6]

Fraught capital–labor relations have been characteristic of capitalism's history. Since Adam Smith, businessmen are known to be pursuing their self-interest, and throughout history, individual tycoons have been notoriously avaricious.[7] But never before had efforts to elevate the current stock price of companies been conducted in such a single-minded, explicit, systematic, and public fashion across an entire economy.

Profit-making for firms and rent-seeking by executives went from being one aspect of capitalism to being the only thing that mattered. The fictional character, Gordon Gekko, in the 1987 movie, *Wall Street*, spoke for many real businessmen when he said: "Greed, for lack of a better word, is good." In

---

[5] J. Bivens and L. Mishel, "Understanding the Historic Divergence between Productivity and a Typical Worker," *Economic Policy Institute*, Report, September 2, 2015, www.epi.org/publica tion/understanding-the-historic-divergence-between-productivity-and-a-typical-workers-pay-why-it-matters-and-why-its-real/; R. Wartzman in *The End of Loyalty: The Rise and Fall of Good Jobs in America* (Public Affairs, 2017) gives a blow-by-blow account of the emergence of the aberration in GE, GM, Kodak, and Coke.

[6] L. Mishel and J. Wolfe, "CEO Compensation Has Grown 940% since 1978," *Economic Policy Institute*, August 14, 2019, www.epi.org/publication/ceo-compensation-2018/.

[7] C. R. Morris, *The Tycoons: How Andrew Carnegie, John D. Rockefeller, Jay Gould, and J. P. Morgan Invented the American Supereconomy* (Times Books, 2006).

The gap between productivity and a typical worker's compensation has increased dramatically since 1979

Productivity growth and hourly compensation growth, 1948–2020

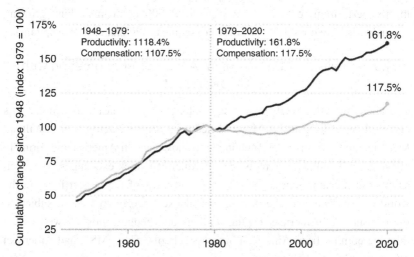

Figure 2 Distribution of productivity gains: Economic Policy Institute
Note: Data are for average hourly compensation of production/nonsupervisory workers in the private sector and net productivity of the total economy. "Net productivity" is the growth of output of goods and services minus depreciation per hour worked.
Source: EPI analysis of data from the BEA and BLS (see technical appendix for more detailed information)

1997, the Business Roundtable (BRT) gave its stamp of approval and boosting the current stock price became the official gospel of American business, until August 2019, when the BRT recognized its error and withdrew its support.[8]

Maximizing shareholder value (MSV) as reflected in the current stock price was not just an esoteric financial practice: it reflected a vast political movement, initially personified by President Ronald Reagan in the United States and Prime Minister Margaret Thatcher in the United Kingdom, and more recently with the corporate tax cuts introduced under President Trump. The political movement lives on in fictions like "corporate tax cuts pay for themselves."[9]

---

[8] "Statement on Corporate Governance," *Business Roundtable*, September 1997, www.ralphgomory .com/wp-content/uploads/2018/05/Business-Roundtable-1997.pdf: "The Business Roundtable wishes to emphasize that the principal objective of a business enterprise is to generate economic returns to its owners"; K. Amadeo, "Greed Is Good or Is it? Quote and Meaning," *Thought & Co*, August 21, 2020, www.thoughtco.com/greed-is-good-or-is-it-quote-and-meaning-3306247.

[9] S. Horsley, "After 2 Years, Trump Tax Cuts Have Failed to Deliver on GOP's Promises," *NPR*, December 20, 2019, www.npr.org/2019/12/20/789540931/2-years-later-trump-tax-cuts-have-failed-to-deliver-on-gops-promises.

MSV not only generated inequality. Ironically, it also had the opposite effect of what was intended. MSV systematically destroyed long-term shareholder value, rather than increasing it. The principal corporate exponents of MSV are mostly performing below the average S&P 500 company. Thus, growing inequality is only one of the negative consequences of shareholder capitalism.

1.5 Capitalism's Aberration: An American Phenomenon with Global Impact

The aberration in capitalism that took place over the last half century was authored by Americans – Milton Friedman, Michael Jensen, and William Meckling and the Business Roundtable. It took place in America and formally affected public companies registered in American stock exchanges. However, as business became increasingly global, and most of the largest firms in the world were registered in the American stock exchanges, they became subject to the pressures of American capital markets and hedge funds, as well as the thinking coming from American business schools. Thus, MSV had American origins, but had global impact.

Further research is needed before we accept the premise that capitalism itself must be totally reinvented. The more modest goal of remedying the current aberration of capitalism based on MSV is more promising and, as explained in later sections, has already begun.

1.6 Capitalism and Creative Destruction

In the 1940s, the political economist, Joseph Schumpeter, described the cyclical nature of capitalism as creative destruction, in which "the process of industrial mutation continuously revolutionizes the economic structure from within, incessantly destroying the old one, incessantly creating a new one."[10]

If Schumpeter is right that capitalism embodies creative destruction, it means that capitalism is inevitably disruptive and economically harmful to all those whose livelihood is tied to arrangements that have become obsolete. The challenge of capitalism is less about reinventing capitalism from scratch, and rather determining how to enhance and share the benefits of capitalism's creative aspects, while rectifying or moderating capitalism's destructive tendencies.

The distinguished economic historian, Carlota Pérez, has provided a brilliant guidebook for accomplishing this in *Technological Revolutions and Financial Capital: The Dynamics of Bubbles and Golden Ages*.[11] Her work builds on

---

[10] J. A. Schumpeter, *Capitalism, Socialism and Democracy* (Routledge, 1994 [1942]), pp.82–83.
[11] C. Pérez, *Technological Revolutions and Financial Capital: The Dynamics of Bubbles and Golden Ages* (Edward Elgar, 2003).

Schumpeter's thinking and shows that "historically technological revolutions arrive with remarkable regularity, and that economies react to them in predictable phases." Thus, capitalism's creative destruction is not merely "one damned thing after another" but rather a predictable series of slow-moving phase changes.[12]

Pérez shows that capitalism has operated for the last 250 years in a recurring pattern of fifty- to seventy-year cycles, following predictable interactions between management, finance, technology, government, and politics.[13] In each cycle, as new technologies emerged, entrepreneurs grabbed the prospect of gain, financiers jumped in, and enormous fortunes were made. Then, after one or more economic crashes, during which income and wealth gaps increased, some groups in the population suffered as others advanced, existing employment was threatened, and trust in institutions crumpled. Such setbacks did not signify the collapse of capitalism, but rather the predictable consequences of capitalism's destructive aspects.

When governments responded wisely at such tipping points, a golden age of broad-based and balanced welfare ensued. If not, inequality and social discord worsened. Today, many countries are at this tipping point, where inequality within countries is deteriorating and politics is increasingly divisive. Autocratic leaders are emerging. Unless worsening inequality is addressed, entire countries may decline, and even disintegrate into chaos.

1.7 The Advent of Customer Capitalism

In the first 150 years of capitalism, there was little discussion of the purpose of a firm. Companies were owned by businessmen-entrepreneurs who preferred the practical challenge of building their business to theorizing about their firm's purpose. But in the early twentieth century, the advent of joint stock companies, the emergence of professional managers to run them, and the risk of those managers diverting the firm's money into their own pockets, led to the question: what purpose should these managers pursue?

The pivotal idea that the purpose of a firm begins with customers came from the management guru, Peter Drucker, who wrote in 1954: "There is only one valid definition of business purpose: to create a customer."[14] Only one. Drucker submitted the idea as a plausible narrative. It was not based on a quantitative study of existing firms. At the time, there were no such firms to study. It was Drucker's theorizing as to what *should* be the purpose of a firm, given his

---

[12] W. Brian Arthur of the Santa Fe Institute: "I thought that the history of technology was – to borrow Churchill's phrase – merely 'one damned thing after another.'"

[13] See also R. Dalio, *Changing World Order: Why Nations Succeed and Fail* (Simon & Schuster, 2021).

[14] P. Drucker, *The Practice of Management* (Harper and Brothers, 1954), p. 98.

understanding of the dynamic of companies under capitalism. Making money was a result, not the goal of the firm.

For the next half-century, firms largely ignored Drucker's idea. As part of their public relations statements, firms often declared that "our customers are number one" and indeed, most firms did what they could for their customers within the limits of their existing structures and processes. But mostly, as explained in Section 7, firms after the 1970s increasingly pursued MSV – maximizing profits for the company, its shareholders, and its executives. Customers were not usually number one.

But in the twenty-first century, customer capitalism took off for four reasons. First, power in the marketplace shifted from seller to buyer, as customers had more choices in the emerging digital economy and better information about those choices.

Second, customers' wishes proved difficult to predict. Merely improving what the firm had delivered before or responding to what customers said they wanted didn't work. Empathy for customers was necessary to understand real needs – needs that customers might not even know they had, such as the iPhone's touchscreen keyboard.[15]

Third, customers increasingly demanded products and services that could make life easy, convenient, cheaper, more fun, or more meaningful, along with increasing disdain for products and services that didn't.

Fourth, the exponential array of digital technologies that are increasingly available in the twenty-first century helped instigate, accelerate, and enable, the management practices of customer capitalism.

1.8 Customer Capitalism: A Different Kind of Management Thinking

Many managers and analysts fail to grasp that the advent of customer capitalism involves much more than a decision to prioritize one class of stakeholder over another within the firm's existing structure and modus operandi. In fact, customer capitalism is built on a different kind of thinking, that leads to new structures, new ways of operating, and requires new kinds of leadership.

In the industrial era of the twentieth century, management thinking reflected an internal view of the firm. Management was about making the firm operate more efficiently and effectively within a relatively stable world, with given systems, processes, and practices. The firm did what it could for the customer

---

[15] S. Denning, "How Empathy Helped Generate A \$2 Trillion Company," *Forbes.com*, July 18, 2021, www.forbes.com/sites/stevedenning/2021/07/18/how-empathy-helped-generate-a-two-trillion-dollar-company/.

within the constraints of its existing systems. Top management knew best and issued directives to the rest of the organization, using steep chains of command to ensure order. Car companies competed against other car companies, banks with other banks, and so on. Managers saw themselves as solving the equivalent of familiar jigsaw puzzles. If they could fit the pieces together into the correct pattern, they could extract, and take, the value they believed to be their due.

Customer capitalism and its management practices embody different thinking. The perspective is mainly external. Success depends less on the internal workings of the firm and more on its ability to master a turbulent unpredictable world of exponential technological possibilities and to delight unpredictable customers. Innovation is pivotal and involves not merely improving what already exists, but creating what is new. The firm aspires to generate new possibilities of working, operating, interacting, playing, and living, for its customers. In the process, the firm can create new experiences for them, just as artists create works of art. Staff and partners are active in the creative process, not mere executors of management's commands. Competition can come from anywhere. The firm is not merely copying or learning known rules. Profits are emergent effects of invention and creation. They are the results of making rather than taking, often out of literally nothing but the imagination.

1.9 How the New Kind of Management Thinking Emerged

Initially, this new management thinking was of little interest to established managements. It began to take hold first in software development following the Agile Manifesto of 2001, which offered a set of priorities and principles as a better way of developing software.[16]

In time, as the digital age unfolded and developing software became steadily more important, customer-centric thinking began spreading from the IT department to running the entire firm, eventually transforming almost every facet of management, as is shown in Section 4 and Figure 16.[17]

In January 2010, management guru Roger Martin announced to the world in *Harvard Business Review* (*HBR*) that a new era – customer capitalism – had begun.[18] And in 2011, the financial sector grasped that "software is eating the world."

Today, it is increasingly becoming apparent that firms embracing the new, more agile ways of creating value for customers, can move more quickly,

---

[16] "Manifesto for Agile Software Development," 2001, https://agilemanifesto.org/.

[17] M. Andreessen, "Why Software Is Eating the World," *Wall Street Journal*, August 20, 2011., www.wsj.com/articles/SB10001424053111903480904576512250915629460.

[18] R. Martin, "The Age of Customer Capitalism," *Harvard Business Review*, January 2010, https://hbr.org/2010/01/the-age-of-customer-capitalism.

operate more efficiently, mobilize more resources, attract more talent, and use it more effectively, win over customers more readily, and enjoy more elevated market capitalizations. Accordingly, the most successful exponents of customer-capitalism have become the most valuable firms on the planet, while former giants, like IBM and GE, which persisted with industrial-era thinking and management, went into steep decline (Figure 3)

1.10 Customer Capitalism: A Different Kind of Leadership

Such deep-seated changes require leadership shifts at the very top of the organization. Merely telling people what to do, or delegating implementation to lower levels, or throwing money at the problem, have turned out to be ineffective.[19] Leaders must exemplify the new way of thinking and the modus operandi in their own conduct. Instead of controlling and containing, they must become inspiring and energizing.

As compared to the grind of bureaucracy in the industrial era, the new approach – with the love for customers and the use of self-organizing teams – was a nice surprise. It could potentially free the human spirit in the workplace from the dispiriting tyranny of a money-hungry hierarchy, while also making companies more productive for customers and for society. The idea of delighting customers had resonance with the other-directed thinking of age-old ethics, in sharp contrast to the self-centered avarice explicit in MSV.[20]

While no firm fully reflects all the aspirations of customer capitalism in everything it does, there is an increasingly sharp divide between the financial results of firms that embrace customer primacy and those of firms that doggedly continue as hierarchical bureaucracies.[21] This steadily growing gap ensures the continuing spread of customer capitalism, despite the disruption to established management practice.

1.11 Capitalism and the Digital Age

Customer capitalism has been fostered and accelerated by exponentially evolving digital technologies. A new economic landscape is being created. As with prior transitions from one era to another, the digital age creates and destroys.

---

[19] See the example of JP Morgan Chase at S. Denning, "What JPMorgan Must Do to Get the Stock Market's Respect," *Forbes.com*, May 30, 2022, www.forbes.com/sites/stevedenning/2022/05/30/what-jpmorgan-must-do-to-get-the-stock-markets-respect/.

[20] S. Denning, "How to Reconcile Management and Morality in Today's Gilded Age," *Forbes.com*, June 22, 2022, www.forbes.com/sites/stevedenning/2022/06/22/how-to-reconcile-management-and-morality-in-todays-gilded-age/.

[21] S. Denning, "Why Your Mission Statement Must Include Customer Primacy," *Forbes.com*, May 22, 2022, www.forbes.com/sites/stevedenning/2022/05/22/why-your-mission-statement-must-include-customer-primacy/.

It generates new opportunities, new markets, and new value, while hastening the obsolescence of almost everything we used to do. As with prior transitions, the new age harms those not able to embrace the change or master its implications.

Digital technology enables the creation of value that is more specific to a customer's need, and more immediate, than ever before. Although digital technology first appeared in the 1940s, beginning in the twenty-first century, the public started to experience value that is instant, frictionless, intimate, and incremental, at scale, and free, or nearly free. That was rarely the case in the industrial era.

To many, digital technology was magic. Very quickly, digital transformed how we work, how we communicate, how we get about, how we shop, how we play and watch games, how we deliver health care and education, how we raise our children, how we entertain ourselves, how we read, how we listen to music, how we watch theater and movies, how we worship; in short, how we live. The transition was accelerated by the ongoing COVID-19 pandemic that began in 2020.

At the same time, we learned that digital technology can also have potentially devastating negative effects. It can be used to create tighter and more minute monitoring and control than even the worst tyrant, while invading without permission every nook and cranny of individuals' private lives, and turning human connections into zombie-like interactions, as customers and employees find themselves dealing with robotic machines rather than people.

When the product itself is digital, some firms have grown very quickly and attained global reach within a few years. In the industrial era, such a rate of growth wasn't possible and such scope had usually taken decades. In digital firms, many of the diseconomies of scale – the difficulties that came from being big – have tended to disappear. Instead, global scale – and the firm being the best in the world at what it did – have started to become almost mandatory for major corporations.[22]

In the digital age, radically different business models have become possible and even necessary: from markets to platforms and ecosystems; from ownership to access, from workers to co-creators of value, from sellers and buyers to providers and users.[23]

Firms that mastered the requirements of the new age have benefited from what economists call network effects. Users get more value as other users join the network, both as an increase in the value to all other users and as an encouragement of nonusers to join the network. In the industrial era, network

---

[22] Wang, R. Everybody Wants to Rule the World: Surviving and Thriving in a World of Digital Giants, HarperCollins, 2021.

[23] J. Rifkin, *The Zero Marginal Cost Society* (St. Martin's Press, 2014).

effects occurred occasionally – for example, telephone networks. For successful firms in the digital era, network effects are pervasive.[24]

Whereas the industrial era was largely based on scarcity, digital services are based on abundance. Exponential technologies can generate an almost infinite array of digital services. It has become possible to make instant contact and converse with anyone from anywhere, buy anything anywhere, access the entire world's information, listen to almost any piece of the world's music, take, share and view unlimited photographs, and create and stream videos, all at zero, or a near-zero cost.[25] The winning firms are those that have found ways to monetize parts of this blizzard of possibilities.

In the digital age, massive amounts of data have also become valuable assets in themselves. Managing data as an asset with tools such as cloud storage, machine learning, algorithmic decision-making, artificial reality, blockchain, and quantum computing enabled firms to better understand the needs of their actual and potential customers and users, and deliver more value to them. Big data often became the key to increasing market share. By contrast, industrial-era firms typically had limited customer-related data and limited capacity to access, analyze, and adjust their services to take advantage of the data they did have.[26]

When the management practices of customer capitalism combined with the array of digital technologies that became available in the twenty-first century, the gains could go from incremental to exponential.[27]

The economy of abundance of the digital age also remedied a systemic flaw of industrial-era capitalism. "Capitalism had always managed to extend the outer limits through 'spatial fixes,' expanding the geography of the system to cover nations and people formerly outside of its range," writes economic historian David Harvey.[28] By the twenty-first century, the industrial-era search for further spatial fixes was pushing the planet to a breaking point. The digital age helps solve the problem by providing an almost infinite array of "digital fixes."

---

[24] Schrage, M. "Rethinking Networks: Exploring Strategies for Making Users More Valuable" MIT Research Brief, Vol. 2016.1.

[25] P. Diamandis and S. Kotler, *Abundance: The Future Is Better Than You Think* (Free Press, 2012): https://medium.com/openexo/forget-startups-exos-exponential-organizations-are-the-new-way-to-innovate-32305d628928; https://singularityhub.com/2016/11/22/the-6-ds-of-tech-disruption-a-guide-to-the-digital-economy/; www.energyjustice.net/solutions/factsheet.

[26] www.mckinsey.com/business-functions/mckinsey-digital/our-insights/managing-data-as-an-asset-an interview-with-the-ceo-of-informatica; S. Denning, "How Data Creates Trillion Dollar Firms the Case of Domino's Pizza," *Forbes.com*, July 23, 2021, www.forbes.com/sites/stevenden ning/2021/07/23/how-data-creates-trillion-dollar-firms-the-case-of-dominos-pizza/.

[27] S. Denning, "How to Become a Winner at Exponential Innovation," *Forbes.com*, February 4, 2021, www.forbes.com/sites/stevedenning/2021/02/04/how-to-become-a-winner-at-exponential-innovation/.

[28] D. Harvey, *Seventeen Contradictions and the End of Capitalism* (Oxford University Press, 2014), p. ix.

1.12 The Emergence of Deep Purpose

The dynamic of industrial-era management was all about the brain – measuring and calculating every possible metric, analyzing the past for clues to the future, and studying ratios and relationships. The passion, if any, concerned being rational. Shows of emotion were almost *verboten*. At most, there was talk of mindset. The heart supposedly had no role.

In the twenty-first century, the heart became exposed. Pervasive access to digital information collapsed the distinction between public and private content, and leaders could no longer hide behind press releases. Casual remarks made in private could become headline news. In the low-trust context, unflattering narratives – both true and false – became pervasive in social media. Some leaders began to see that they needed to present themselves and their firms as they are and express honestly what they believe. There has been a growing recognition that the whole person – including the heart – is key to leadership in this emerging world.

Building trust in companies and their leaders isn't easy, given many decades of dissembling. Commerce had become the antithesis of the authentic. Moreover, inside the firm, rah-rah HR workshops compounded the offense by attempting to manipulate the staff's very sense of self, getting them to profess feelings that they had never felt.

Three catastrophes served as wake-up calls. The COVID-19 pandemic underlined the role of government in public health and the private sector recognized its responsibility for inventing vaccines and treating workers right. Working from home created a vast social experiment that accelerated the adoption of technology and digital ways of working. Similarly, the war in Ukraine elicited both unprecedented collaboration between multiple governments, and support from the private sector. Increasingly extreme weather events have underlined the urgency of action to deal with climate change. These events served as warnings for firms to think beyond profit and explore the possibilities of deep purpose and authenticity.

1.13 Fixing the Flaws of the Digital Winners

An inherent aspect of capitalism is that some actors become very wealthy very rapidly, while those that are less able to adapt fall by the wayside. In a winner-take-most world, big firms grow even bigger, and are tempted to unfairly exploit their dominance. In due course, the winners are demonized, while the losers exercise political pressure to prevent change and redress their suffering. These phenomena – familiar to business historians – are now playing out in the emerging digital age and are frequently – and mistakenly – seen as unprecedented.

The lessons of history can be helpful. The accumulation of sudden wealth is not necessarily a sign of wrongdoing. Yet the abuse of newly acquired power is common and must be addressed. Regulations designed for different technologies need to be rethought so as to encourage benefits for everyone while limiting winners' inevitable missteps. Self-regulation by winners to resist the temptation to crush every competitor must be part of the solution.

Current bipartisan efforts to regulate big technology firms have assumed a strident tone. These phenomena are common in the transition from one age to another. The challenge is to understand the facts underlying the claims and counter claims, find ways to depoliticize decision-making, and implement effective regulation.

1.14 The End of Shareholder Capitalism

For the last half century, major firms, particularly in the United States, embraced MSV. Although this virus-like narrative was later called "the world's dumbest idea" by one of its most famous exponents, Jack Welch, the former CEO of GE, the narrative became the official policy of American business, with the 1997 declaration of the Business Roundtable.[29]

Meanwhile, evidence showed that maximizing shareholder value encouraged short-termism and destroyed long-term shareholder value. It also encouraged corporate greed, unfairly depressed worker compensation, prompted grotesque executive compensation, and necessitated the continuance of hierarchical bureaucracy,

Shareholder value thinking is not just obsolete. It is financially, economically, socially, and morally wrong. Yet there are powerful vested interests in keeping things as they are. As Upton Sinclair pointed out a century ago, "It's hard to get a man to understand something when he is being paid not to understand it."

Finally in 2019, several hundred CEOs of major firms signed the Business Roundtable denunciation of shareholder value, and declared support for creating value for all the stakeholders.

Now in mid-2022, almost three years since the Business Roundtable's denunciation of shareholder value, there is scant evidence that firms sought authorization from their boards of directors to change their firms' purpose. Since maximizing shareholder value had been the official purpose of business for several decades, shareholder value is embedded in firms' strategies, systems, processes, values, and practices. Changing all these elements will be a mammoth undertaking. As of now, most big firms have barely begun.[30]

---

[29] F. Guerra, "Welch Condemns Share Price Focus," *Financial Times*, March 12, 2009 www.ft.com/content/294ff1f2-0f27-11de-ba10-0000779fd2ac; S. Denning, "Making Sense of Shareholder Value: 'The World's Dumbest Idea'," *Forbes.com*, July 17, 2017, www.forbes.com/sites/steve denning/2017/07/17/making-sense-of-shareholder-value-the-worlds-dumbest-idea/.

[30] L. Bebchuk and R. Tallarita, "'Stakeholder' Capitalism Seems Mostly for Show," *Wall Street Journal*, August 6, 2020, www.wsj.com/articles/stakeholder-capitalism-seems-mostly-for-show-

In many firms, shareholder value thinking is pervasive but almost invisible to those within the firm. It is part of "the way we do things around here." For companies that have been pursuing shareholder value for decades, it has become a taken-granted basic assumption as to how members of that organization should perceive, think about, and deal with situations and issues. Thus, since maximizing shareholder value remains the de facto goal of many large firms, its eradication requires further work.

1.15 Why Stakeholder Capitalism Leads to Indecision

Despite its flaws, shareholder value thinking is at least an internally consistent way to run an organization. By contrast, stakeholder value thinking – the notion that a firm should focus on adding value to all its stakeholders – is incoherent. Guidance to head in several directions at the same time is inherently problematic as a corporate goal.

The lessons of history are instructive. The narrative of stakeholder capitalism was launched in 1932, by Adolf Berle and Gardiner Means in their book, *The Modern Corporation and Private Property*. It proposed that firms should have professional managers, who would act as trustees and balance the needs of "the owners, the workers, the consumers, and the State," case by case, for the benefit of society. The narrative was pursued for several decades in the mid- twentieth century and had one main problem. It didn't work. An organization attempting it tended to become a morass of indecision, and mid-level managers turned into indecisive Dilbert-like characters.[31]

After shareholder capitalism took over in the latter part of the twentieth century, and making money became the firm's overriding goal, stakeholder capitalism receded in prominence until 2019, when it reemerged in the new Business Roundtable declaration. Informed observers view corporate support for stakeholder capitalism as a façade for continuing MSV.[32] Section 7 shows why reformers who see stakeholder capitalism as a potential cure for corporate greed are pursuing a mirage.

11596755220; R. Henderson, "US Companies Cling to Share Buybacks Despite Collapse in Profits," *Financial Times*, July 30, 2020, www.ft.com/content/1c924be0-5bc0-4eba-a088-b98b13080c04.

[31] S. Denning, "Putting an End to Dilbertian Management," *Forbes.com*, April 26, 2011, www.forbes .com/sites/stevedenning/2011/04/26/putting-a-definitive-end-to-dilbert-style-management/.

[32] L. Bebchuk and R. Tallarita, "'Stakeholder' Capitalism Seems Mostly for Show," *Wall Street Journal*, August 6, 2020, www.wsj.com/articles/stakeholder-capitalism-seems-mostly-for-show-11596755220; J. Unseem, "Beware of Corporate Promises," *The Atlantic*, August 6, 2020, www .theatlantic.com/ideas/archive/2020/08/companies-stand-solidarity-are-licensing-themselves-discrim inate/614947/; www.ft.com/content/1c924be0-5bc0-4eba-a088-b98b13080c04.

1.16 What You Will Learn in This Element

In this Element, you will experience the vast and remarkable drama that has been under way for several centuries – one that has affected the lives of every human being. Capitalism has been a success story for more than 250 years, but now faces fresh challenges.

You will learn that the form of capitalism that we have experienced in the last half century, particularly in the United States, is an aberration from the previous 200 years. It led to the systematic extraction of value for the benefit of one group of actors at the expense of all others. Some aspects of today's perceived crisis in capitalism flow from the consequences of this aberration. A primary challenge facing capitalism today is thus, not to reinvent every aspect of capitalism from scratch, but rather to understand and rectify this particular aberration.

You will learn that today's perceived crisis of capitalism also reflects the normal and predictable tipping point of capitalism's slow moving life-cycle, in which a new group of technologies and management practices has made whole sections of the economy and society obsolete, causing abrupt disruptions, inequalities, and understandable anger.

You will learn from similar moments in history – long before we were born – that when governments take steps in such situations to guide the healthy dissemination of benefits and to restrain the predictable overreach of winners, chaos can be averted, and a golden age of innovation may prevail.

You will learn that today's most widely cited formulation of capitalism – stakeholder capitalism – serves both as an incoherent holy grail sought by reformers and as a smokescreen embraced by corporations to maintain the status quo.

You will learn that the now officially discredited aberration of capitalism of the last half century – shareholder capitalism – is still alive and thriving in the shadows, and continues to generate its noxious consequences.

You will learn that the most successful firms in today's digital age are practicing customer capitalism, in which the co-creation of value for customers and users generates benefits for all the stakeholders; profits are a result, not the goal. You will learn that customer capitalism is a necessary step in getting the benefits needed to address inequality and climate change.

You will learn that most industrial-era firms attempting to implement customer capitalism are struggling in the absence of the necessary deep shift in management practices, attitudes and thinking: such firms find that most of their efforts at digital transformation have not generated the expected benefits.[33]

---

[33] G. F. Davis, *Taming Corporate Power in the 21st Century* (Cambridge University Press, 2022); S. Denning, "Why Digital Transformations Are Failing," *Forbes.com*, May 23, 2021, www.forbes.com/sites/stevedenning/2021/05/23/why-digital-transformations-are-failing/.

In this extraordinary story, you will learn that solutions are not about papering over problems with soft-headed maxims like "doing good in the world" or by demonizing capitalism's winners. They are about becoming more tough minded, both within companies about what works and what doesn't, and within government by taking a fact-based approach to regulating the predictable issues of capitalism's current cycle and addressing climate change.

		Market cap $ billion	5 year growth in stock price	Net income 2021 ($b)	Sector	Founded	Thousands of employees
Average S&P 500			**+77%**				
First generation digital giants							
	Apple	2,290	+316%	101	Multi-sector tech	1976	132
	Microsoft	2,100	+313%	71	Multi-sector tech	1975	166
	Google (Alphabet)	1,560	+156%	76	Technology	1998	135
	Amazon	1,140	+138%	33	Multi-sector tech	1996	1,700
Potential digital giants							
	Tesla	731	+918%	6	Automotive	2003	71
	NVIDIA	429	+373%	10	Software, chips	1993	18
	Salesforce	172	+112%	4	Cloud software	1999	50
Former digital giants							
	Neflix	87	+26%	30	Visdeo streaming	1997	11
	Meta (Facebook)	476	+13%	39	Social media	2004	59
"Digital upstarts "							
	Shopify	46	+343%	3	E-commerce	2006	7
	Etsy	10	+465%	0.5	E-commerce	2005	1
Firms "transitioning to digital"							
	Deere & Co	90	+176%	6	Equipment, agriculture	1837	74
	Target	68	+228%	2	retail	1962	368
Large firms growing faster than the S&P 500 over the past 5 years							
	Costco	210	+227%	6	Retail	1976	288
	United Health	469	+189%	17	Health, insurance	1977	330
	Progressive	64	+207%	2	Insurance	1937	35
	LVMH	309	+157%	12	Luxury goods	1923	158
	Sony	103	+125%	9	Media conglomerate	1946	112
	Home Depot	283	+109%	16	Retail hardware	1978	400
	Pfizer	281	+94%	22	Phamacuticals	1849	79
	Procter & Gamble	341	+87%	15	Consumer products	1837	101
	American Express	109	+89%	8	Financial services	1850	65
	Walmart	339	+79%	14	Retail	1976	2,200
Large firms growing slower than the S&P 500 over the past 5 years							
	Merck	233	+74%	13	Pharmaceuticals	1891	68
	Bershire Hathaway	590	+66%	90	Insurance	1955	360
	Cisco Systems	182	+62%	12	Technology	1984	78
	Bank of America	258	+54%	31	Banking	1998	213
	JP Morgan	345	+53%	42	Banking	2000	257
	Marriott	46	+43%	1	Hotels	1927	121
	Exxon	359	+40%	14	Oil	1999	72
	Volkswagen	87	+39%	18	Automotive	1937	663
	Netflix	81	+26%	5	Movies, video	1997	9
	Ericsson	26	+18%	2	Telecommunications	1876	99
	GM	59	+14%	10	Automotive	1908	157
	Wells Fargo	144	-11%	21	Banking	1852	233
	Michelin	20	+3%	2	Tires	1889	127
	AT&T	148	+1%	20	Telecommunications	1983	230
	SAP	102	+0%	5	Software, chips	1972	107
	Unilever	117	+0%	7	Food, health	1894	149
	Electrolux	4	-24%	1	Appliances	1919	52
	IBM	125	-38%	6	Technology	1924	346
	GE	71	-67%	-7	Multisector	1892	205

Figure 3 Financial landscape, June 25, 2022

1.17 The Financial Landscape as of June 2022

Figure 3 ranks public companies by the five-year-growth of their total shareholder value. It reflects the view that a principal goal of all forms of capitalism is to create long-term shareholder value. It enables comparisons of progress towards that goal, as against the average for all S&P 500 companies.

It is a forward-looking measure, incorporating the combined judgment of the stock market as to the future shareholder value of each company. In this respect, it differs from indices like the Fortune 500 which ranks firms by way of the backward-looking measure of total revenue.

It is also a measure that enables the relative performance of firms in terms of growing value to be evaluated against other firms. The measure is to a certain extent subject to the vagaries of the stock market, the contagious narratives predicting booms or busts, and investors' gaming of the system. However, a comparison of the long-term total return of firms against the average S&P 500 firm can help to evaluate the scale and relevance of such vagaries, since contagious narratives have a limited life expectancy, and the relative rankings of firms over a period of five years generally remain quite stable.

It is striking that many of the large famous old firms demonstrate modest growth paths, while the strongly performing firms tend to be proponents of customer capitalism.[34]

---

[34] The rankings that emerge from an analysis of the growth of market capitalization are remarkably similar to the rankings that emerge from the qualitative methodology of "The Management Top 250 ranking," developed by the Drucker Institute, which "measures corporate effectiveness by examining performance in five areas: customer satisfaction, employee engagement and development, innovation, social responsibility, and financial strength." *Wall Street Journal*, December 11, 2021, www.wsj.com/articles/explore-management-top-250-11639167806?mod=article_inline.

2 The Overall Shape of Capitalism

2.1 Why the World Is Better and Why Almost No One Knows It

This section explains the overall shape of capitalism's dynamic. The first snapshot from 2017 examines the popular narrative that everything is getting worse. It presents data showing that this is not so. The popular but wrong assumption risks distorting analysis and recommendations towards the negative. The article was first published in Forbes on November 30, 2017.[35]

Read the news and you can see that the world is going to hell in a hand-basket – and fast! Terrorism, nuclear weapons, economic stagnation, social unrest, autocratic leaders, structural unemployment, de-skilling, growing hopelessness, the opioid epidemic, increasing inequality, xenophobia, economic migrations, recessions, financial bubbles and crashes, recessions, depressions – the list goes on.

So, when a recent survey asked, "All things considered, do you think the world is getting better or worse?" the results were predictably bleak. In Sweden only 10% thought things are getting better. In the United States, it was only 6%. Hardly anyone thinks the world is improving.

In a powerful study entitled "The short history of global living conditions and why it matters that we know it" by Oxford economist Max Roser, the founder of *Our World in Data*, we learn that on virtually all of the key dimensions of our material well-being – poverty, literacy, health, freedom, and education – the world is a much better place than it was a couple of centuries ago.[36]

2.1.1 Poverty

Even the Bible tells us that "The poor, you will always have with you." And it's customary to see poverty as so intractable that organizations aiming to reduce global poverty, like the World Bank, might as well try boiling the ocean. Statistics show otherwise. Massive gains have been made in reducing extreme poverty, particularly in the last fifty years. Some countries that are now rich were poor just a few decades ago.

Two centuries ago, only a privileged few were not living in extreme poverty. For all the ills of industrialization, increased productivity steadily lifted people out of extreme poverty. At first, the progress was modest: in 1950, 75% were still living in extreme poverty. But today, those living in extreme poverty are now less than 10%.

This is an extraordinary achievement, particularly because the world population has increased seven-fold over the last two centuries. Vital goods and

---

[35] S. Denning, "Why the World Is Getting Better," *Forbes.com*, November 30, 2017, www.forbes.com /sites/stevedenning/2017/11/30/why-the-world-is-getting-better-why-hardly-anyone-knows-it/.

[36] https://ourworldindata.org/a-history-of-global-living-conditions-in-5-charts.

services became more plentiful: more food, better clothing, better housing, and indoor plumbing.

Amid the flurry of bad news in the media, it's easy to miss how far and how fast we have come. As the media are obsessed with reporting events where things have gone wrong, it is easy to overlook the extraordinary fact shown in Figure 4: "since 1990, on average, there were 130,000 people fewer in extreme poverty every single day."

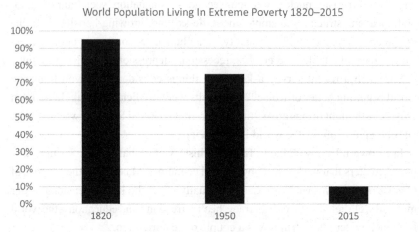

Figure 4 World poverty

Source: *Our World in Data*

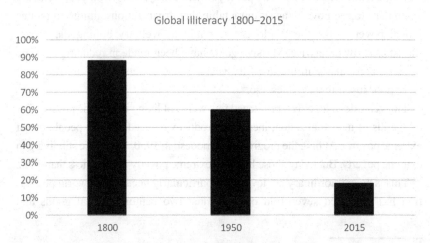

Figure 5 Global trends in literacy

Source: *Our World in Data*

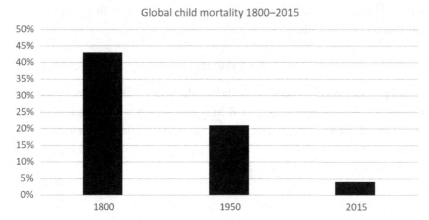

Figure 6 Global trends in health

Source: *Our World in Data*

2.1.2 Education and Literacy

The education story is just as encouraging. Data show that the share of the world population that is literate has, over the last two centuries, gone from a tiny elite to a world where eight out of ten people can read and write, as shown in Figure 5.

2.1.3 Health

Progress in health is equally astonishing. A key reason for our surprise? We don't know how bad things used to be. In 1800, more than 40 percent of the world's newborns died before the age of five. Now only a tiny fraction dies before the age of five, as shown in Figure 6. How come? Modern medicine helped, particularly the discovery of germs, but even more important were improvements in housing, sanitation, and diet.

2.1.4 Freedom

Political freedom also made progress. Given the emergence of populist leaders and dictators around the world, it's easy to underestimate what's happened in establishing political freedom and civil liberties, which are "both a means for, and an end of, development."

Freedom is notoriously hard to measure, and *Our World in Data* uses as an index of democracy "the least problematic of the measures that present a long-term perspective." This index suggests that in the nineteenth century almost everyone lived in autocratically ruled countries.

Our World in Data cites various estimates and concludes that more than half the global population now lives in a democracy, as shown in Figure 7. "The huge majority of those living in an autocracy – four out of five – live in one autocratic country: China."[37]

2.1.5 Population

World population was around one billion in the year 1800 and increased seven times since then, as shown in Figure 8. In one sense, this is a great achievement. Better health means that humans stopped dying at the rate of our ancestors. In effect, "humanity started to win the fight against death. Global life expectancy doubled just over the last hundred years."

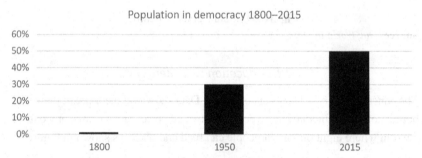

Figure 7 Global trends in democracy 1800–2015
Source: *Our World in Data*

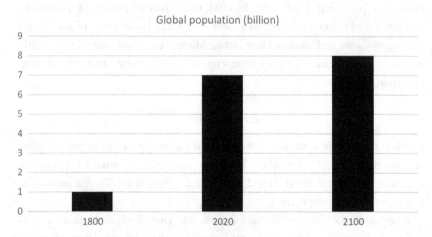

Figure 8 Population
Source: *Our World in Data*

---

[37] https://ourworldindata.org/democracy.

In another sense, though, population growth increased demand for resources and aggravated humanity's impact on the environment. But population growth isn't unlimited. "Once women realize that the chances of their children dying has declined substantially, they adapt and choose to have fewer children. Population growth then comes to an end."

All these gains were enabled by improvements in knowledge and education. *Our World in Data* forecasts that education will continue to improve. "With today's lower global fertility, the researchers expect that the number of children will decline from now – there will never be more children on the planet than today." World population should peak in 2070 and to decline thereafter. "With the great importance of education for improving health, increasing political freedom, and ending poverty, this projection is very encouraging."

2.1.6 Why Don't We Know the World Is Getting Better?

It's ironic that in a world where knowledge and education are improving dramatically, there is widespread misunderstanding of the improving state of the world. "More than nine out of ten people do not think that the world is getting better."

Our World in Data suggests that the media are partly to blame. The media do not tell us how the world is changing; it tells us where the world is going wrong. It focuses on single events that have gone bad. By contrast, positive developments happen slowly with nothing to promote in a headline. "More people are healthy today than yesterday," just doesn't cut it.

2.1.7 The Challenges Ahead

Obviously, big problems remain. Having one out of ten people living in extreme poverty today is unacceptable. Humanity's impact on the environment is unsustainable. Continuing threats to political freedom must be dealt with. Future gains are by no means assured. Remaining problems will be hard to solve.

The picture painted by these statistics is also technocratic and global in perspective. It is no solace to an individual family that is suffering to learn that the global picture of human welfare has improved over several centuries. If we talk to the people moved from their land by force or driven into tall apartment buildings, it is no comfort to learn about rising income counted in dollars if prices are rising faster. Human value and values are not adequately reflected in a spreadsheet.

Yet there are grounds for cautious optimism.

First, the fact that future progress is hard to predict doesn't make it unlikely. Thus, it's hard to imagine anyone in the year 1800 forecasting the progress that would be made over the next two centuries. Today, pessimists have the megaphone and predict almost certain doom for humanity, because this is what gets attention. Yet could that all be part of humanity's stumbling effort towards bettering itself?

Second, although harder challenges lie ahead, we now know much more about the solutions. For instance, we know that the key to population limits is getting people out of poverty: above $10,000 per capita, population growth drops precipitously. Paradoxically, one key to saving the environment is growing incomes faster!

Third, global poverty reduction has been a success. But when people believe that they are failing, they risk losing faith in each other. Greater awareness of our history can build confidence to tackle the remaining problems.

Fourth, we have learned much about collaboration. International institutions and global compacts have been set up. Track records exist. "Solving problems – big problems – is always a collaborative undertaking . . . We have just seen the change over time; the world today is healthier, richer, and better educated."

Fifth, we now know more about how to adapt. The idea that we should do things today as we did them yesterday has given way to a realization that if further progress is to be made, we must learn to adapt even faster. Bureaucratic practices that aim at preserving the status quo are bottlenecks to achieving further progress. Innovation must be continuous. In a world of accelerating change, and increasing complexity, organizations must learn how to become more agile.

2.2 From a Casino Economy to a New Golden Age

The second snapshot in this section, also from 2017, provides a guidebook on managing the "creative destruction" of capitalism. It presents the distinguished economic historian, Carlota Pérez and the findings of her path-breaking book, Technological Revolutions and Financial Capital: The Dynamics of Bubbles and Golden Ages *(2002).*[38]

The book builds on Joseph Schumpeter's theory of the link between innovation and financial dynamics. In it, Pérez lays out a history of five technological revolutions that follow a similar pattern of boom, bust, and in some cases, renewal.

---

[38] W. Brian Arthur, Santa Fe Institute, on reading Pérez: "I thought that the history of technology was – to borrow Churchill's phrase – merely 'one damned thing after another.'"

Capitalism is thus not something that happens willy-nilly, with booms and busts occurring randomly. Capitalism happens in fifty to seventy-year cycles that can and must be managed at each stage. In the early phases of the cycle, the government should be mainly hands off. In the clean-up phase, when inevitable inequalities have emerged and over-reach by the winners is occurring, governments must step in. Otherwise, the economy will careen towards disaster.

The relevance for today is that many countries are now at this tipping point where inequality within countries is worsening, and politics is increasingly divisive. Autocratic leaders are becoming prominent. Unless remedial action is taken to address the obvious problems of worsening inequality and climate change, economies may decline and disintegrate into chaos.

Since 2017, three new crises – the COVID-19 pandemic of 2020, the war in Ukraine of 2022, and increasingly extreme weather events – have underlined both the urgency and the possibilities of international collaboration.

This article was first published in Forbes.com on October 25, 2017.[39]

When Carlota Pérez, the distinguished economic historian, finished speaking last week at the Drucker Forum, her talk elicited a sustained round of applause.

That's because Pérez drew on decades of research, decoded economic problems that trouble us all, and pointed to a clear path forward. Whereas most of us think that 20 years is a long-term perspective, Pérez takes a 240-year horizon. In so doing, she shows us patterns that are not visible when we look at what has happened in our lifetimes.

Mark Twain allegedly said that history doesn't repeat itself, but it does rhyme. In effect, Pérez's work shows us what rhymes in the last 240 years of economic history.

Instead of history being just "one damn thing after another," Pérez shows us that we are actually living through repeating longer-term cycles. In this way, the options – and consequences of different decisions – become much clearer. Here's her talk.

Carlota Pérez: It is time for government to come back boldly, wisely, and adequately. In saying this, I know that I'm swimming against the tide. But what I am saying is solidly grounded in the history of technological revolutions and the associated role of finance.

[39] S. Denning, "From Casino Economy to a New Golden Age," *Forbes.com*, November 25, 2017, www.forbes.com/sites/stevedenning/2017/11/25/from-a-casino-economy-to-a-new-golden-age-carlota-perez-at-drucker-forum-2017/.

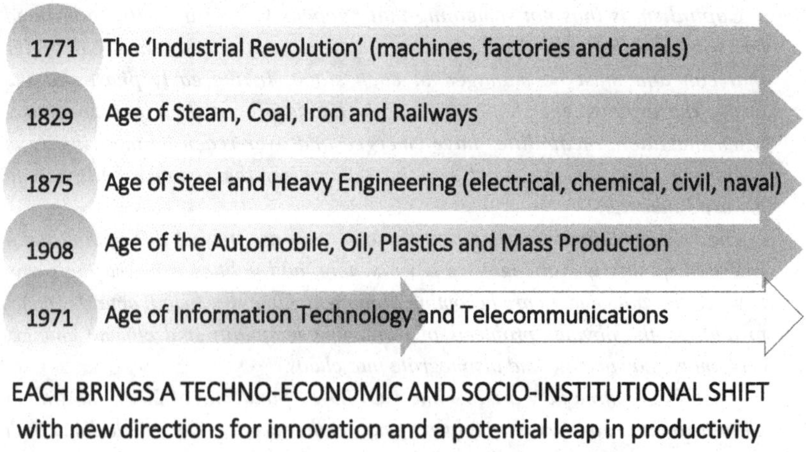

1771	The 'Industrial Revolution' (machines, factories and canals)
1829	Age of Steam, Coal, Iron and Railways
1875	Age of Steel and Heavy Engineering (electrical, chemical, civil, naval)
1908	Age of the Automobile, Oil, Plastics and Mass Production
1971	Age of Information Technology and Telecommunications

EACH BRINGS A TECHNO-ECONOMIC AND SOCIO-INSTITUTIONAL SHIFT
with new directions for innovation and a potential leap in productivity

Figure 9 Five technological revolutions in 240 years

2.2.1 Five Technological Revolutions

To summarize: there have been five technological revolutions over the last 240 years, as shown in Figure 9 (in this, I follow Schumpeter's lead, rather than some recent interpretations, which count two, three, or four).

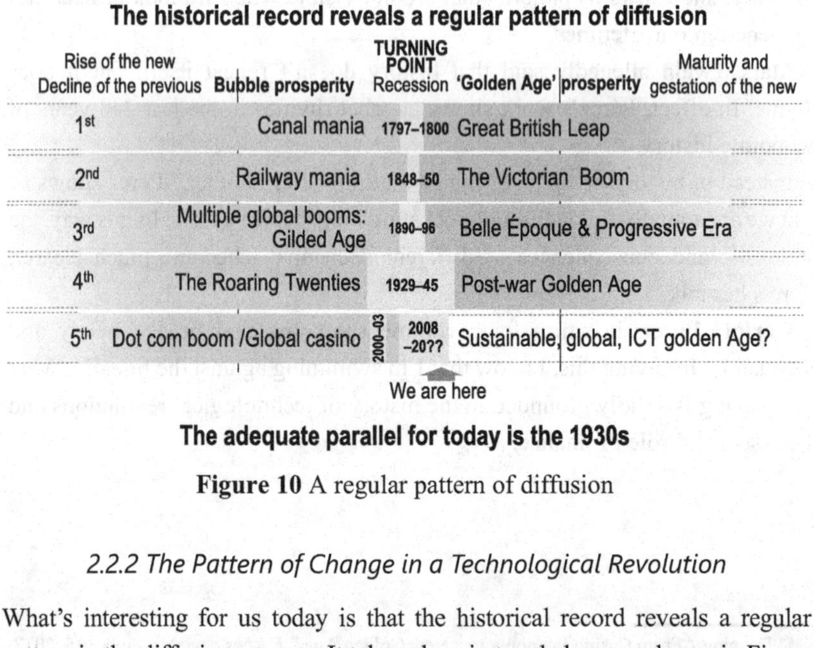

The historical record reveals a regular pattern of diffusion

	Rise of the new / Decline of the previous	Bubble prosperity	TURNING POINT Recession	'Golden Age' prosperity	Maturity and gestation of the new
1st		Canal mania	1797–1800	Great British Leap	
2nd		Railway mania	1848–50	The Victorian Boom	
3rd		Multiple global booms: Gilded Age	1890–96	Belle Époque & Progressive Era	
4th		The Roaring Twenties	1929–45	Post-war Golden Age	
5th		Dot com boom /Global casino	2000–03 2008 –20??	Sustainable, global, ICT golden Age?	

We are here

The adequate parallel for today is the 1930s

Figure 10 A regular pattern of diffusion

2.2.2 The Pattern of Change in a Technological Revolution

What's interesting for us today is that the historical record reveals a regular pattern in the diffusion process. It takes place in two halves, as shown in Figure 10. First, we have the rise of the new technology that occurs during the decline of the previous revolution. It's like the 1980s, when we had inflation with the old technologies, which were yielding decreasing returns, while the information technology companies were growing fast with steadily increasing returns (and decreasing prices).

That first half is the installation period of the new technology, which leads to, and ends with, one or more bubble prosperities – as in the late 1990s and mid-2000s – when the financial sector and the casino economy take over.

Then the bubble or bubbles burst, and we have a recession, that might last from two to thirteen years or more.

That recession phase is what I call "the turning point," because it is the time when the control of investment shifts from finance to production, normally with the aid of the State. When that has happened in the past, we have experienced strong growth in a kind of Golden Age, with broad-based prosperity.

But the Golden Age cannot continue forever. Returns from the new technology start to decline. Then comes the inevitable maturity of that technological revolution and the process starts all over again.

2.2.3 The Sequence of Changes: The Role of the Turning Point

In the first Industrial revolution, we had the Canal Mania and then the Canal Panic during the Napoleonic Wars, leading to the great British leap forward.

Then we had the Railway Mania and the subsequent Railway Panic, when it became apparent, as in each case, that there had been over-investment. After a short recession, came the Victorian boom times of the 1850s and 1860s in the United Kingdom, with capitalist Britain increasingly assuming global leadership.

Then the Age of Steel, from the 1870s onwards, led to multiple global booms – in the United States Germany, Australia, New Zealand, South Africa, and Argentina – as massive global opportunities led to an investment boom. Everyone wanted to participate. That is, until a series of crashes came in various forms across the world.

Chastened by the crashes, the financial sector in the United States and Germany returned its focus to funding the real economy, which stabilized the situation. The result was less happy for Argentina, which ceased to be a major player in the world economy. Great Britain concentrated on globalization and empire, rather than investing enough in electricity, steel, and the new chemicals. So, it began losing its leadership position in the global economy. Once again, the change involved a great deal of waste and pain, but the financial sector had funded the infrastructure for the new global economy.

From the late 1890s, came a period of relative calm and prosperity, with the Belle Époque in Europe, and the Progressive Era in the United States, in which monopolies were broken up and issues of income inequality were addressed.

The fourth revolution – Mass Production – led to massive investment and growth in the Roaring Twenties until the Crash of 1929, which in turn led to the Depression of the 1930s. This period was a long turning point of thirteen years, which paved the way for a period of broad-based prosperity, including the Second World War, which taught business the advantages of working with government.

Then from 1970 onwards, we have the age of Computers and Tele-communications. The mid-1990s, when government handed over the Internet to business, saw rapid economic growth, ending in the Dot.com crash in 2000 and then the casino economy of the mid-2000s, with the collapse across the world of various bubbles in housing and synthetic financial instruments.

2.2.4 The Current Turning Point

Now in 2022, we are in the middle of another turning point. As in the 1930s, we could have a period of sustained global prosperity if appropriate action is taken, as shown in Figure 11.

As in the 1930s, we have structural unemployment, low investment, growing inequality, a sense of hopelessness, risk-averse finance with trillions of dollars sitting on the sidelines, feeble growth, social unrest, recessions, and talk of secular economic stagnation. Populist leaders find massive followings,

Figure 11 The Postwar Golden Age

precisely because of these issues. They exploit the rampant xenophobia against subgroups. It could be the Jews or the Muslims. Somebody must be at fault, and large-scale economic migrations further aggravate xenophobia.

Despite these problems, there was then, and is now, a huge underlying technological potential, but the potential cannot be realized without a clear, common, synergistic direction.

That is why now is the right historical moment for the government to come back on the scene, boldly, actively, and wisely. In a turning point, government is not the problem: government is the solution.

This is what eventually happened in the 1940s. Government action and the Second World War led to mass production and mass consumption. Large numbers of people had access to relatively cheap products. Suburbanization made it profitable for firms to innovate for the family in the electric home with its insatiable hunger for new products. At the same time, the Cold War led to government investment in high tech. The reconstruction of Europe also stimulated economic growth and the demand for equipment and other goods.

The welfare state enabled mass consumption. That's one reason why high taxes were possible without resistance. The top rate was around 90 percent throughout the 1950s. The money went out of tax-payers' pockets, passed through the hands of government, and came back as solvent demand for consumer goods or procurement. Firms prospered because they were able to pursue an agreed common vision of what "the good society" looked like and what innovation was needed to make it happen. Everyone was going to have a home with cheap appliances. Credit was available that enabled people to buy

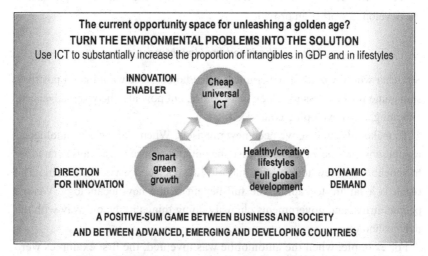

Figure 12 The current opportunity for a Golden Age

houses and goods. It was an intelligent positive-sum game between government, business, and society, which led to the greatest economic boom in history.

2.2.5 A New Positive-Sum Game: Green Growth?

Moving on to our own time, we can see that there are new possibilities for an intelligent positive-sum game. The ongoing technological revolution based on computers and telecommunications has immense potential benefits for everyone. Yet there are also risks. We are facing environmental issues: not just global warming and pollution, but also a scarcity of natural resources. We cannot give every Chinese and Indian person the American Way of Life: we simply don't have seven planets.

What to do? We need to turn our environmental problems into economic solutions, as shown in Figure 12. We need to use information technology to increase the proportion of intangible services available world-wide. We need Internet access everywhere, both universal and cheap. The direction for innovation is clear: smart, green growth. This of course will mean changes in lifestyle, just as we have seen changes in lifestyles in all previous technological revolutions. The technology generates the new possibilities, and the new needs provide dynamic demand. The adoption of new lifestyles leads to jobs that replace those eliminated by the ongoing technological revolution. The new jobs enable widespread prosperity.

The other dimension of increasing demand today is the economic growth needed, not just in China and India, but in all of Asia and Africa and Latin America. Full global development would both improve the lives of the majorities and provide demand for capital goods, engineering and all the things that the developed world can provide.

2.2.6 The Need for New Mindsets

So, what would we get if government acted boldly? We would get a positive-sum game for business and society as before, but now also between advanced, emerging, and developing countries.

To make this happen, we need new mindsets. Whenever these technological revolutions have occurred in the past, the initial response has always been to try to shoehorn the new technology into old lifestyles and ways of thinking. The result is a failure to capture the full benefit of the new technology. We see people, firms, and governments clumsily doing things in the old way with the new technology.

For example, when the automobile was invented, the first examples were like motorized versions of a horse and cart. It took time for people to grasp

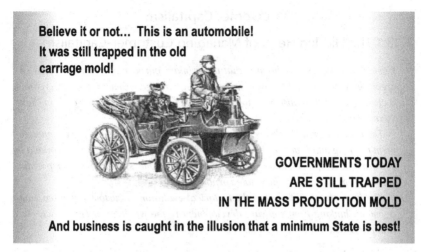

Figure 13 Trapped in the wrong mental model

the possibilities of the new technology, independently of what had gone before, as shown in Figure 13.

We face similar issues today. Governments are still trapped in a mass-production mindset, while business is trapped in the illusion that minimal government is best. If we are going to achieve economic growth with greater income equality and sustainable well-being, we need to get out of both traps and work together.[40]

---

[40] Attention should also be paid to the work of Oxford University Professor Colin Mayer in terms of rethinking the definition of profit to include environmental concerns: www.forbes.com/sites/karlmoore/2022/03/22/rethinking-the-purpose-of-business-with-oxford-professor-colin-mayer/.

3 Customer Capitalism

3.1 The Hidden Heart of Managing Customer-Capitalism

Customer capitalism is the idea that the primary purpose of a firm concerns co-creating value for the customer. Wordings range from a mere "creating a customer," to "an obsession to create value for the customer," or even to "love your customer as yourself."

The two snapshots in this section shed light on how customer-focused management thinking and practices had a difficult birth but eventually gained a foothold in software development and then, as software became steadily more important, spread from software to the whole corporation.

The first snapshot describes the historical evolution of customer-focused management thinking from software development to the whole firm. This article was first published in Forbes.com on November 5, 2018.[41]

When did modern management begin and where is it heading? A case can be made that it was born with Peter Drucker's 1954 insight: "There is only one valid definition of business purpose: to create a customer."[42]

Like many great insights in human history, when this thought came into the world, no bells were rung, no celebrations were held, and no Nobel prizes were awarded. There were solemn nods to Drucker's lengthy tome, but little more.

That's because Peter Drucker's brilliant idea ran contrary to what humans had assumed at least since Adam Smith, namely, that the purpose of a firm is to make money. It was as obvious as the fact that the sun revolves around the earth, until we discovered that it wasn't so.

3.1.1 Why Management Baulked at Drucker's Insight

In management, Drucker's insight was ignored. Rather than embracing it, theorists in the 1970s, and firms in the 1980s, doubled down on the opposite proposition. Business schools and public corporations embraced the notion that the purpose of a firm is to maximize shareholder value as reflected in the current stock price. This led to the disasters of excessive financialization and short-termism.

Because boosting the stock price so as to make money for the shareholders and the executives was not a goal that naturally inspired those doing the work, firms had to use command-and-control methods to *require* workers to execute the goal. In effect, shareholder value locked in bureaucracy, which in turn blocked progress towards the continuous

---

[41] S. Denning, "The Hidden Heart of 21st Century Management," *Forbes.com*, November 25, 2018, www.forbes.com/sites/stevedenning/2018/11/25/lets-celebrate-the-hidden-heart-of-21st-century-management/.

[42] P. Drucker, *The Practice of Management* (Harper and Brothers, 1954), p. 98.

innovation that firms would need to succeed in the emerging digital age.[43]

More recently, as firms saw the necessity of having an inspired workforce, multiple Ideas started cropping up to rethink management. There were various labels, including innovation management, design thinking, Agile management, the experience economy, blue ocean strategy, humanocracy, humanistic management, the Rendanheyi model, and more. The ideas were useful, but fell short rethinking the overall purpose of the firm and its role in integrating multiple functions.

When we look beneath these labels, we can detect a common thread related to putting Drucker's insight into practice. This is not surprising: work, firms, and management are inherently about *human beings creating more value for other human beings*. Rather than adding fresh labels, we need a radically distilled message that draws attention to the essence of what's involved.

3.1.2 An Idea Whose Time Has Come

Fortunately, Peter Drucker's insight is an idea whose time has finally arrived. As a result of shifts in the marketplace – the accelerating pace of change, the increasing complexity, and the shift in power from seller to buyer – firms that deliver increasing value to customers are now flourishing. They have a radically different kind of management with three key elements, or "laws" that were born in software development and then spread to the whole firm to enable business agility and continuous innovation:

- An obsession with co-creating value for *customers* as the existential goal of the organization.
- A presumption that work should be done in self-organizing teams, working in short cycles and focused on delivering value to customers.
- An interacting network of teams, rather than a steep command-and-control hierarchy.[44]

This way of managing enabled both operational agility – making the existing business better – and strategic agility – generating new products and services

---

[43] S. Denning, "Wall Street Costs the Economy 2% of GDP Each Year," *Forbes.com*, May 31, 2015, www.forbes.com/sites/stevedenning/2015/05/31/wall-street-costs-the-economy-2-of-gdp-each-year/; S. Denning, "Resisting the Lure of Short-Termism," *Forbes.com*, January 8, 2017,www.forbes.com/sites/stevedenning/2017/01/08/resisting-the-lure-of-short-termism-how-to-achieve-long-term-growth/.

[44] S. Denning, "Explaining Agile," *Forbes.com*, September 8, 2016, www.forbes.com/sites/stevedenning/2016/09/08/explaining-agile/.

and bringing in new customers.[45] In substance, the management model was the foundation for firm-specific terminology, labels, processes, and brands of the most successful firms of the digital era. In the best-run firms, HR, budget, planning, strategy, and finance systems were also aligned to reflect and enhance these elements, as shown in Figure 16.

When firms took seriously the idea of creating value for customers, and aligned their management practices with this goal, they made more money more quickly than any firms in history.[46] Those that haven't mastered the shift are often struggling. As a result, this way of working is fast becoming a commercial necessity. Those who continue to think that the goal of business is to make money don't understand either business or making money.

The option facing most organizations today is stark. They will either embrace Peter Drucker's insight and align their entire management with it, or they will struggle and eventually perish. Change or die. It's as basic as that.

3.2 The Triumph of Customer Capitalism

The second snapshot in this section describes the emergence of customer capitalism and explains its epochal meaning by analogy to the Copernican revolution in astronomy. It explores the reasons why firms have had difficulty in making the shift from resolving complicated issues to solving complex problems.
This article was first published in Forbes.com on January 10, 2020.[47]

Like most foundational ideas – such as honesty, integrity, or accountability – that are the basis of a prosperous society, customer capitalism isn't a shiny new object with a fancy label, just discovered by money-seeking consultants, hawking the next new management gadget.

Nor is customer capitalism a secret. For those with eyes to see, it is as plain as day. The most successful firms today proclaim loudly and clearly that they are pursuing what Peter Drucker long ago saw to be "the true North" of a corporation: creating value for customers.[48] Generating fresh value for customers is the basis for generating benefits for *all* the stakeholders, not *vice versa*.

[45] S. Denning, "Beyond Agile Operations: How to Achieve the Holy Grail of Strategic Agility," *Forbes.com*, February 10, 2017, www.forbes.com/sites/stevedenning/2017/02/10/beyond-agile-operations-how-to-achieve-the-holy-grail-of-strategic-agility/.

[46] S. Denning, "Why Agile Is Eating the World," *Forbes.com*, January 2, 2018, www.forbes.com/sites/stevedenning/2018/01/02/why-agile-is-eating-the-world%E2%80%8B%E2%80%8B/#6665fe4f4a5b.

[47] S. Denning, "The Triumph of Customer Capitalism," *Forbes.com*, January 10, 2020, www.forbes.com/sites/stevedenning/2020/01/10/the-triumph-of-customer-capitalism/.

[48] S. Denning, "Drucker vs World's Dumbest Idea," *Forbes.com*, May 2018, www.forbes.com/sites/stevedenning/2018/05/30/peter-druckers-virtuous-firm-vs-the-worlds-dumbest-idea/.

To be sure, Drucker noted that successful corporations need to take care of many other things besides customers, including safety, legality, profitability, sustainability, great workplaces, respect for the community, the environment, and so on. But the purpose, the overriding goal, and the very *raison d'etre* of the firm, to which the firm must single-mindedly direct its efforts if it is to thrive, is to give primacy to creating customers.

3.2.1 We Live in an Age of Customer Capitalism

The realization of Drucker's vision of 1954, and its emergence as "customer capitalism," was announced in January 2010 by the "Vatican of management," *Harvard Business Review*, in the article, "The Age Of Customer Capitalism," written by management guru, Roger Martin, the former Dean of the Rotman School of Management at the University of Toronto.[49]

Martin writes:

> "Modern capitalism can be broken down into two major eras. The first, managerial capitalism, began in 1932 and was defined by the then radical notion that firms ought to have professional management. The second, shareholder value capitalism, began in 1976. Its governing premise is that the purpose of every corporation should be to maximize shareholders' wealth. If firms pursue this goal, the thinking goes, both shareholders and society will benefit. This is a tragically flawed premise, and it is time we abandoned it and made the shift to a third era: customer-driven capitalism."

Drucker's customer capitalism is a moral posture. It is the opposite of the institutionalized greed implicit in the current aberration of capitalism, namely, to make money for shareholders and executives, at the expense of everyone else. Loving your customer as yourself is an ethical, other-directed concept. It puts people at the center of the firm. It reconciles money and morality. It is a different world from today's aberration of capitalism – maximizing the current stock price.

The shift from shareholder capitalism to customer capitalism is not simply an adjustment of the calculus by which firms measure their success. It entails a different mental model of how the world works. The shift is as fundamental in scope and implications as the Copernican Revolution in astronomy.

---

[49] R. Martin, "The Age of Customer Capitalism," *Harvard Business Review*, January 2010, https://hbr.org/2010/01/the-age-of-customer-capitalism.

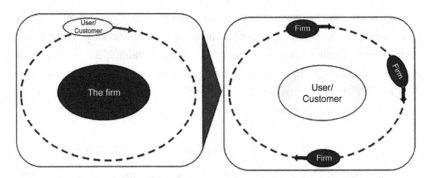

Figure 14 The Copernican revolution in management

3.2.2 The Copernican Revolution in Astronomy

On the surface, the Copernican Revolution in astronomy was no more than a simpler way for astronomers and astrologers to calculate the paths of the planets. Instead of thinking of the Sun as revolving around a stationary "center of the universe" – the Earth – Copernicus said that we needed to think of the Earth as one of numerous planets revolving around the Sun.

Yet hidden within this innocuous notion about the mechanics of the planets was a radically different idea of the relationship of the universe to the human world. The notion would in due course undermine the plausibility of established religion in general, the Roman Catholic Church in particular, and the Divine Right of Kings, on which most governments in Europe rested their claim to legitimacy. Copernicus's theory, first published in 1543, thus began an inexorable process of inquiry into the entire organization of society. Understandably, the inquiry was resisted by the powers-that-be. Several centuries went by before it was fully accepted.

3.2.3 The Copernican Revolution in Management

Similarly, on the surface, customer capitalism is the simple idea that a firm needs to pay attention to the customer because it is the customer who generates the firm's revenue and hence ensures its survival. Yet, as with the Copernican Revolution in astronomy, embedded within customer capitalism is a different vision of how the world works, as shown in Figure 14.

At the heart of customer capitalism today is the recognition that the world has changed. Power in the marketplace has shifted from the seller to the buyer. Abruptly, frighteningly, and to the surprise of the powerful command-and-control executives of big firms, the customer is now the boss.

Globalization, deregulation, and new technology, particularly the Internet, have provided the customer with choices, reliable information about those choices and the ability to interact with other customers. Suddenly the customer expects value that is instant, frictionless, intimate, interconnected, and preferably free. Now firms thrive only so long as they are nimble enough to adapt to customers' shifting needs and desires better than the many other firms vying to do likewise. The result? A Copernican Revolution in management.

3.2.4 The Results of Customer Capitalism

Twelve years after Martin's article, the results of the customer-capitalism revolution are in. The largest and fastest growing firms on the planet are those that are obsessed with delivering value to customers. Their names are famous: Alphabet (Google), Amazon, Apple, and Microsoft. They had a combined market-capitalization of some $4 trillion in early 2020 (and double that two years later). All of these firms have flaws, which need to be addressed. But these firms also demonstrate the extraordinary money-making capability of co-creating value for customers.[50]

The principal reason for their success is that they have delivered to customers the current gold standard of corporate performance: quicker, easier, more personal, more connected value that is cheaper, and preferably free.

3.2.5 The Necessary Transformation of Management

If the financial gains are so great, why don't all firms commit to customer capitalism and deliver the gold standard of corporate performance? Why are so many big businesses, the World Economic Forum, and the Business Roundtable, wasting their time with the already-failed notion of stakeholder capitalism?

It turns out that implementing customer capitalism is not as simple as it looks. Delivering the new corporate gold standard of performance entails a transformation of every aspect of management, as shown in Figure 16. The slow-moving command-and-control bureaucratic management of the industrial-era is incapable of meeting the needs of customers who want things "now, just for us, with no hassle, compatible with what we have already, wherever and whenever we want it."

Embedded in customer capitalism is a different worldview, which threatens the hegemony of all hierarchical bureaucracies that systematically dispirit those doing the work, frustrate those for whom the work is done, repeatedly disappoint society and yield increasingly meager returns for investors.

---

[50] S. Denning, "Six Lessons on Agile," *Forbes.com*, June 27, 2018, www.forbes.com/sites/steve denning/2018/06/27/six-lessons-that-society-must-learn-about-agile/.

Customer capitalism has thus begun an inquiry into the contribution of command-and-control bureaucrats who currently preside over large organizations in both the public and private sectors. It shreds the assumption that these executives are value-creating entrepreneurs, worthy of extraordinary compensation. It invites a reexamination of the duties, rights, and privileges of all those who happen to be occupying these often extravagantly paid positions.

3.2.6 A Journey into the World of the Customer

The shift in the center of the corporate universe from firm to customer is a radical idea. As the economist Hunter Hastings points out:

> "Value is in the mind of the customer. It's an experienced benefit, a feeling, an emotion. That's why it's called subjective. If value is in the customer's mind, then firms can't 'create value' (business school lingo) and there is no such thing as 'shareholder value.' Firms can create customers, and they do so by facilitating the customer's value experience. Meeting the needs of customers lies entirely in the customer domain."[51]

This is a domain that the command-and-control management of the industrial-era is unfamiliar with.

3.2.7 A Shift from Complicated to Complex

A domain that management can control – the internal workings of the firm, its processes, systems, and modalities – is very different from a world in which the customer is the boss. The command-and-control world of shareholder capitalism is complicated. It is predictable. It operates in a linear fashion. It can be governed by routines and processes. It can ignore how human beings feel about things. The command-and-control corporation is a machine that grinds relentlessly onward.

Bureaucracies, the executives who run them, and the business schools that teach them, are often more comfortable solving the complicated problems of these command-and-control machine-like organizations than they are understanding and mastering the complex, interactive context of customer capitalism, where the world is governed by the all-too-human values, attitudes, feelings, and dreams of both customers and those delivering the value.

Dealing with complexity means grappling with uncertainty and the need to be adaptive and agile, to learn by doing, and to respond to feedback. The

---

[51] H. Hastings, "The New Economics of Value and Value Creation," *Economics for Business*, March 29, 2021, https://econ4business.com/the-new-economics-of-value-and-value-creation/.

discomfort in dealing with complexity is one reason why executives have been slow to do what is necessary to embrace customer capitalism.

Too often, business assumes a complicated world of linear change, which can be analyzed and predicted. In a complex setting, that is not the case, even in principle. Instead, the organization needs to be gathering information, taking exploratory steps, seeing what reactions occur, and adjusting, as shown in Figure 15.

		The difference between complicated and complex systems		
		Complicated systems	Complex systems	Implication
I.	Causality	Linear cause-and-effect pathways	No clearly distinguishable cause-and-effect pathways	Root cause analysis is mostly a waste of time
2.	Linearity	Every output of the system has a proportionate input	Outputs are not related in a linear fashion to inputs	Tiny changes can have massive impact
3.	Reducibility	The system can be decomposed into its structural parts	The parts create change in one another in unexpected unpredictable ways	High levels of surprise, uncertainty, even from merely observing the system
4.	Controllability	Contexts and interactions can be controlled; problems can be diagnosed and permanently solved	Emergent patterns obscure the real problem. Small interventions have disproportionate consequences	System can't be deconstructed into its component parts, fully understood, optimized, and fixed
5.	Openness	System is closed and can only interact with selected types of systems	System is open, making it impossible to separate from its context.	Ignore the system's context at your peril!
6.	Knowability	System can be deconstructed and fully known or modeled.	System cannot be fully known no matter how much data are collected	The only way to understand system is to interact with it.
7.	Adaptability	System needs an external force to introduce change.	System can observe itself, learn, and adapt.	Complex systems can actively resist change

Figure 15 The difference between complicated and complex systems
Source: Sonja Blignaut "Seven Differences between complex and complicated"

These are difficult lessons, but ones that the entire economy is now having to learn. As Kodak, Blockbuster, Nokia, GE, and many others discovered, the message is simple: change or die.

4 The Digital Age

4.1 What Is the Digital Age and What Does It Mean?

This section points to the reality that developed economies are not merely entering a new phase of the industrial era, but rather a wholly new age – the digital age.

The digital age has already created a great divide. On one side, some firms are generating immense benefits for customers and users, while reaping extraordinary rewards for themselves, as shown in Figure 3. *On the other side, many big firms are pouring resources into digital investments but struggling to get proportionate returns.*[52]

The success stories have not depended on the relative size of IT budgets. Nor are they confined to "born digital" organizations like Alphabet, Amazon, Nvidia and Tesla. Older firms like Apple and Microsoft have also succeeded in creating the management, leadership and innovation mindset that are needed. The winners succeed by "democratizing" leadership throughout the firm.[53] *Top-down siloed bureaucracies lack the agility to succeed in the digital economy.*

The digital age is not a future event. The first snapshot shows that the transition to a new age is already happening on a massive scale. It has transformed almost everything we do. Yet we are still at the beginning. What lies ahead is potentially so large that the whole canvas is difficult to grasp.[54] *This article was first published in Forbes.com on February 8, 2022.*[55]

As books like *Dignity In The Digital Age* (2022) by Congressman Ro Khanna appear, talk of "the digital age" becomes commonplace, and executives grapple with "digital disruption" as their top management challenge. Yet there is little agreement as to what exactly is "the digital age," or what it means.[56]

4.1.1 The Birth of the Industrial Era

Some light can be shed on the confusion by looking at the arrival of the last great age, the industrial revolution, several centuries ago. Even in retrospect, historians don't agree as to what we mean by "the industrial revolution."

---

[52] M. Iansiti and S. Nadella, "Democratizing Transformation," *Harvard Business Review*, May–June 2022, https://hbr.org/2022/05/democratizing-transformation; S. Denning, "What JPMorgan Must Do to Get the Stock Market's Respect," *Forbes.com*, May 30, 2022, www.forbes.com/sites/stevedenning/2022/05/30/what-jpmorgan-must-do-to-get-the-stock-markets-respect/.

[53] M. Iansiti and S. Nadella, "Democratizing Transformation," *Harvard Business Review*, May–June 2022, https://hbr.org/2022/05/democratizing-transformation.

[54] S. Denning, "Fresh Critiques of Agile," *Forbes.com*, July 12, 2020, www.forbes.com/sites/stevedenning/2020/07/12/dealing-with-fresh-critiques-of-agile/.

[55] S. Denning, "What Is the Digital Age?" *Forbes.com*, February 9, 2022, www.forbes.com/sites/stevedenning/2022/02/09/what-is-the-digital-age-and-what-does-it-mean/.

[56] R. Khanna, *Dignity in the Digital Age* (Simon & Schuster, 2022).

Some historians see it primarily as an economic phenomenon that began in Britain, starting with mechanized spinning in the 1780s, and only reaching the rest of Europe by the mid-nineteenth century. Others see it as an *engineering* and *technological* phenomenon, with high rates of growth in steam power and iron production occurring after 1800. Some analysts see it as the beginning of *management* as a field of expertise. Some writers see it as an offshoot of *improved agricultural productivity* that freed up agriculture workers to be employed elsewhere in the economy. Others adopt *a gradualist perspective* and suggest that there was no sudden transformation at all, but rather *a confluence of many factors* over several centuries. Each discipline tends to pursue its own perspective as "the" way to understand the industrial revolution, thus distracting from the fact that the era was the result of "all of the above."[57]

The arrival of the industrial era was traumatic. It tore lives and workplaces apart, upended existing businesses, destabilizing the agricultural economy and existing political systems. It shattered old values, challenged old power relationships, the privileges of the elites, and created the space where the power struggles of tomorrow were to be fought.[58]

4.1.2 Adam Smith and Wealth of Nations (1776)

In the 1770s, describing all the implications of the industrial revolution would have meant telling the lords and ladies living in luxury on their grand manors and agricultural estates, with their tenant farmers touching their forelocks as these aristocrats drove by in their elegant horse-drawn carriages, that they were going to be replaced by crass upstart businessmen, who would be tearing their aristocratic world apart, driving the tenant farmers off their estates and into the cities to undertake boring repetitive work known as "jobs."

Even less plausible would be telling the lords and ladies of their eventual destiny in the new age as tour guides of their grand manors for the hoi polloi, and becoming quaintly comic figures in television series like *Downton Abbey.*

The Scottish philosopher and economist, Adam Smith, took a stab in *Wealth of Nations* (1776), but even he foresaw only a sliver of it. A lot had yet to happen before the scope of the industrial revolution could be grasped. A factory that made pins more efficiently was interesting, but at the time, hardly headline news.

Even so, *Wealth of Nations* covered a lot of ground. It was part economics textbook, part management textbook, part finance textbook, part social

---

[57] M. Overton, *Agricultural revolution in England: The Transformation of the Agrarian Economy 1500-1850.* (Cambridge University Press, 1996), https://archive.org/details/isbn_9780521568593.

[58] A. Toffler, *The Third Wave* (Random House, 1984), p. 10.

commentary, and part futurology. It was the best that could be done with a phenomenon as overwhelming as a new age.

Almost by definition, any book that tried to describe it all would not have fitted into any existing category of book. If *Wealth of Nations* had attempted it, it would never have had the impact that it had. It was because the book was multifaceted that readers could begin to sense the possibilities of what had just begun.

After several decades, the landscape clarified. People sensed a revolution. Thus, in 1813, the Scottish statistician Patrick Colquhoun wrote in "*A Treatise on the wealth, power and resources of the British empire*" (London, 1813):

> "It is impossible to contemplate the progress of manufactures in Great Britain within the last thirty years without wonder and astonishment. Its rapidity, particularly since the commencement of the French revolutionary war, exceeds all credibility. The improvement of the steam engines, but above all the facilities afforded to the great branches of the woolen and cotton [manufactures] by ingenious machinery, invigorated by capital and skill, are beyond all calculation; these machines are rendered applicable to silk, linen, hosiery, and various other branches."

By the early 1800s, the well-to-do were beginning to experience the impact of the new era in their lives, although it would be another half century before the average citizen would see major gains.

4.1.3 Explaining the Digital Age

Today, with the emerging new age that is most commonly called "the digital age," each book or article has covered fragments of the whole. There is writing on the amazing new technologies that are now available.[59] There is writing on how our lives are being transformed.[60] There is writing on aspects of the management changes that are needed to succeed with those technologies.[61] There is writing on how corporate finance has been transformed.[62] There is writing on how individual sectors have been affected.[63] There is writing on the

[59] S. Denning, "How to Become a Winner," *Forbes.com*, February 4, 2021, www.forbes.com/sites/stevedenning/2021/02/04/how-to-become-a-winner-at-exponential-innovation/.

[60] S. Denning, "Golden Age of Innovation," *Forbes.com*, September 19, 2021, www.forbes.com/sites/stevedenning/2021/09/19/why-we-live-in-a-golden-age-of-innovation/.

[61] S. Denning, "Reinventing Management," *Forbes.com*, February 26, 2011, www.forbes.com/sites/stevedenning/2011/02/26/reinventing-management/.

[62] S. Denning, "Why the Economy Will Be Run by Digital Giants," *Forbes.com*, July 21, 2021, www.forbes.com/sites/stevedenning/2021/07/21/why-the-entire-economy-will-be-run-by-digital-giants/.

[63] S. Denning, "How Volvo Embraces Agile at Scale," *Forbes.com*, January 26, 2020, www.forbes.com/sites/stevedenning/2020/01/26/how-volvo-embraces-agile-at-scale/.

potential gains that are available, as well as on the failure of many existing firms to take advantage of those opportunities, resulting in "digital disruption."[64] There is writing on the different culture of the successful firms.[65] There is writing on the need to update economics to incorporate what is happening.[66] There is writing on the missteps of the digital winners and the risks of the new age, and what should be done to regulate the negative impacts.[67] There is futurist writing that talks about where this is all heading.[68]

What is lacking, and what is needed, is writing that presents a coherent picture of all the various aspects of the new age in a way that it can be understood, and dealt with, rationally, in its entirety.

4.1.4 The Transition to the Digital Age

A new age is thus upon us, and firms are not blind to the riches being heaped on the digital winners. As a result, most firms are firms pouring money into the new technology with digital initiatives and Agile transformations. Armies of consultants have been happy to train large numbers of staff on the new digital technologies. Yet without deeper change in obsolete industrial era mindsets, those digital technologies are unlikely to generate much benefit. Success in the digital age requires different levels of agility and integration, along with a passionate obsession with delivering value to customers.

The industrial-era mindset, built on the goal of maximizing shareholder value, is still prevalent in large corporations, along with the attendant principles and processes that follow from it – bureaucracy, vertical hierarchy, autocratic leadership, backward looking strategy, sales and marketing focused on short-term profit, and control-oriented HR. Corporations run in this fashion cannot adapt and integrate their activities fast enough to get the benefit from digital technologies.

---

[64] S. Denning, "Why Digital Transformations Are Failing," *Forbes.com*, May 23, 2021, www.forbes.com/sites/stevedenning/2021/05/23/why-digital-transformations-are-failing/.

[65] A. Steiber, *Management in the Digital Age: Will China Surpass Silicon Valley?* (Springer, 2017); A. Steiber, *Leadership for a Digital World: The Transformation of GE Appliances* (Springer, 2022).

[66] R. Chainey, "Beyond GDP: Time to Rethink How We Measure Growth," *World Economic Forum*, June 4, 2016, www.weforum.org/agenda/2016/04/beyond-gdp-is-it-time-to-rethink-the-way-we-measure-growth/.

[67] S. Denning, "Why Big Tech Should Regulate Itself," *Forbes.com*, August 2, 2020, www.forbes.com/sites/stevedenning/2020/08/02/why-big-tech-should-regulate-itself/.

[68] S. Denning, "Why the Economy Will Be Run by Digital Giants," *Forbes.com*, July 21, 2021, www.forbes.com/sites/stevedenning/2021/07/21/why-the-entire-economy-will-be-run-by-digital-giants/.

In effect, until companies start to have a frank discussion of the currently undiscussable subject of the underlying assumptions as to how they are run, it will be hard for them to be successful in the digital age.

4.2 A Powerful Diagnostic Tool for Digital Era Enterprises

The second snapshot in this section offers a diagnostic tool to measure the progress of the transition from industrial-era management to operating in the digital age. It can be used at the level of the firm, a unit, a team, or an individual. The article was first published in Forbes.com on January 3, 2021.[69]

There are currently two strikingly different ways of running a corporation in a coherent and consistent fashion. In one – the predominant mode of the industrial era, refined over the last fifty years – the goal of the firm is to make money for the firm and maximize shareholder value. This goal leads to principles and processes that emphasize stable structures that control staff, contain costs, and increase revenues, profits and the current stock price. This approach was successful in the relatively stable industrial era and is still applicable in some contexts.

By contrast, for digital era management – the pioneering mode of Agile enterprises and of leading Silicon Valley firms, as well as individual businesses in Europe and China – the goal of the firm is to create customers.[70] This goal leads to principles and processes that enable agility as well as stability. The principles and processes help firms mobilize talent to create instant, intimate, frictionless, incremental value for customers. In this mode of operating, profits and the stock price are viewed as results, not goals.

The new management is thus very different from the industrial era. Instead of a focus on internal efficiency and outputs, the primary preoccupation in the new age is external: an obsession with creating value and outcomes for customers and users.[71] Instead of starting from what the firm can produce that might be sold to customers, digital firms work backwards from what customers need and then figure out how that might be delivered in a sustainable way.[72] Instead of

---

[69] S. Denning, "A Powerful Diagnostic Tool for Agile," *Forbes.com*, January 3, 2021, www .forbes.com/sites/stevedenning/2021/01/03/a-powerful-diagnostic-tool-for-agile-enter prises/.

[70] S. Denning, "How Amazon Became Agile," *Forbes.com*, June 2, 2019, www.forbes.com/sites/ stevedenning/2019/06/02/how-amazon-became-agile/; S. Denning, "Drucker Forum, 2018," *Forbes.com*, December 2, 2018, www.forbes.com/sites/stevedenning/2018/12/02/drucker-forum-2018-post-bureaucratic-management-at-vinci-and-haier/.

[71] S. Denning, "How Customers Made Microsoft a Two Trillion Dollar Company," *Forbes.com*, June 25, 2021, www.forbes.com/sites/stevedenning/2021/06/25/how-customers-made-microsoft-a-two-trillion-dollar-company/.

[72] S. Denning, "Strategy Means Working Backwards," *Forbes.com*, September 30, 2021, www.forbes .com/sites/stevedenning/2021/09/30/why-strategy-now-means-working-backwards-from-the-future/.

limiting themselves to what the firm itself can provide, the firm often mobilizes other firms to help meet user needs.[73] Instead of leadership located solely at the top of the organization, leadership and initiative that create fresh value are nurtured throughout the organization.[74] Instead of tight control of individuals reporting to bosses, self-organizing teams throughout the firm create value by working in short cycles and drawing on their own talents and imagination.[75] Instead of the steep hierarchies of authority of industrial era-firms, digital firms tend to be organized in horizontal networks of competence.[76] In these ways, most of the central management tenets of the industrial era have been upended.

Firms operating in the new way have been transforming everything society does – how we work, play, shop, access knowledge, learn, entertain ourselves, communicate, move about, stay healthy and even how we worship. For better or worse, our lives are becoming as different from those of the industrial era as those of the industrial era were different from the agricultural age. Firms that are able deliver these kinds of benefits have enjoyed massive financial gains and astronomic market capitalizations.

As a result, most firms see the writing on the wall and recognize in varying degrees that the old way of operating can't cope with the current disruption. Most are pursuing transitions from the old to the new at various speeds and intensities. Yet most of these efforts are no more than partial steps towards digital-era management. The result is generally a mishmash of industrial-era and digital-age principles and processes that is no more effective in coping with the disruption than trying to run from a tsunami crashing onshore.

The principles and processes of the two modes of management are not merely different. In most cases, they are the opposite of each other. Moreover, because the principles and processes in each system of management mutually support each other, they tend to operate like the body's immune system: the proponents of each process help defend the organization against deviations from the norm. If an inconsistent process appears, the overall system will tend to combine and treat the deviant process like an invading virus that must be destroyed and eliminated from the organization.

Thus, for firms practicing industrial-era management, the principles and processes of digital age management, such as self-organizing teams and networks of

---

[73] S. Denning, "Ecosystem Firms," *Forbes.com*, April 18, 2021, www.forbes.com/sites/stevedenning/2021/04/18/why-ecosystem-firms-are-the-future-of-management/.

[74] S. Denning, "Leading Change from Anywhere," *Forbes.com*, March 21, 2021, www.forbes.com/sites/stevedenning/2021/03/21/how-to-lead-change-from-anywhere/.

[75] S. Denning, "Eight Keys to Unleashing Your People," *Forbes.com*, February 28, 2021, www.forbes.com/sites/stevedenning/2021/02/28/eight-keys-to-unleashing-your-people/.

[76] S. Denning, "Don't Reorganize: Use an Agile Network," *Forbes.com*, June 7, 2020, www.forbes.com/sites/stevedenning/2020/06/07/dont-reorganize-run-your-firm-as-an-agile-network/.

competence can be seen as a threat to the stability and top-down control of industrial-era management. It is only when the principles and processes of an organization are entirely aligned with either the industrial-era or the digital-age modality that the firm will be free from internal infighting and friction.

4.2.1 A Diagnostic Tool: The Principles and Processes Worksheet

The Principles and Processes (PP) worksheet is an analytic tool that can help firms diagnose their status in relation to the two systems of management. It can be applied either to the entire organization or to any part of that organization, such as the leadership team, or any unit, or any team, or even an individual, at any point in time. Differences between viewpoints can also be measured. The tool is shown in summary form in Figure 16.

The tool provides a kind of MRI scan of the organization. With the use of the tool, managers can see at a single glance the health of their organization, or any part of it, along with clear implications as to where the problems are and how to go about fixing them.

Without such a diagnostic tool, managers and consultants, risk making the effects of market disruption worse, with actions such as CEO firings, down-sizings, delayerings, reorganizations, and efficiency drives. Such managers and consultants don't intend harm: they take those steps because they have no way of making an objective assessment of the state of the organization or the organizational dysfunctions that need treating.

4.2.2 Using the Diagnostic Tool

The PP worksheet enables leaders to map where industrial-era or digital-age principles are being practiced, in their own business unit, entire organization, or leadership team. Each of these assessments is likely to be different in the details. Those using the PP worksheet will become what Richard Sheridan, CEO of Menlo Innovations, calls "high tech anthropologists" probing what is going on.[77] The worksheet can also be used to compare different viewpoints on the same unit.

For example, the PP worksheet in Figure 17 has been used to picture retroactively what happened in a major Silicon Valley organization over a twenty-year period. At the outset, as shown in 1998, the firm was implementing industrial-era management. After several years with a new CEO, the firm was making progress towards digital-age management, as shown in 2000.

---

[77] S. Denning, "The Joy of Work: Menlo Innovations," *Forbes.com*, August 2, 2016, www .forbes.com/sites/stevedenning/2016/08/02/the-joy-of-work-menlo-innovations/.

Principles and processes of Industrial-Era and Digital-Age firms.			
A. Principles: What is driving actual behavior in the organization?			
A. Principles	Industrial-Era management	⬅━━━➡	Digital-Age management
1. Goal	Making money for the firm and its shareholders	O—O—O—O—O	Obsession with creating more value for customers and users
2. Profits	Primary goal of the firm	O—O—O—O—O	Profits are the result of a sustainable business model, not the goal of the firm
3. Structure of work	Individuals report to bosses, fill roles	O—O—O—O—O	Drawing on full talents of staff, with small self-organizing teams
4. Dynamic	Vertical hierarchy of authority	O—O—O—O—O	Horizontal network of competence
5. Key indicator: Short-term	Delivering short-term profits	O—O—O—O—O	Delivering instant, intimate, frictionless value for customers
6. Key indicator: Long-term	Current stock price	O—O—O—O—O	Multi-year rate of growth of market capitalization
B. Processes that support the above principles			
7. Leadership	Leadership from the top; transactional	O—O—O—O—O	Leading occurs at every level; inspirational
8. Strategy	Static, backward looking, building moats	O—O—O—O—O	Dynamic, interactive, value-creating strategy; ecosystems
9. Environment and social goals	Doing what is necessary	O—O—O—O—O	Making an above-average contribution
10. Innovation	Protecting and growing the existing business	O—O—O—O—O	Enhancing the existing business and creating new businesses
11. Sales & marketing	Inducing customers to buy the firm's current products	O—O—O—O—O	Making a difference for customers and users
12. People management	HR controlling workers as the firm's disposable resources	O—O—O—O—O	Attracting and enabling talent to add value to customers and users
13. Operations	Making output targets at lower cost	O—O—O—O—O	Exceeding expected outcomes at lower cost
14. Measurement	Measuring internal outputs against what was promised	O—O—O—O—O	Measuring external outcomes against what was envisaged
15. Budget	Silos battling for resources for their unit	O—O—O—O—O	Budget reflecting and enhancing decisions already taken in strategy
16. Risk management	Risk management viewed as neutralizing threats	O—O—O—O—O	Managing risk as opportunity
17. Compensation	Top takes the lion's share of any productivity gains	O—O—O—O—O	All staff paid for the value they help create, including productivity gains

Figure 16 Principles and processes worksheet

Some ten years after that, the firm under the same CEO had essentially completed the transition to digital-age management as shown in 2014, along with a major expansion of revenues.

However, a change in the senior management shortly thereafter sparked a return to industrial-era management. After several years, the reversion was visible, as shown in 2000, and was accompanied by a significant decline in revenues.

Without the PP worksheet, all that observers could say was that the CEO holding office in the time period covered in 2000 and 2014 was a better executive than his predecessor or his successor. With the help of the PP worksheet, we can grasp the specific performance issues and accomplishments at each stage, along with pointers as to how the firm can redress the underlying causes of the decline in performance.

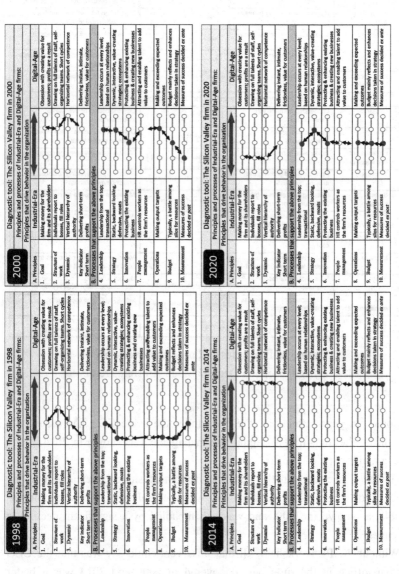

Figure 17 Transition of a firm over time

5 The Emergence of Deep Purpose

5.1 What Firms Must Learn about Deep Purpose

This section sketches how issues of authenticity and the heart are coming to play a key role in modern capitalism. Affirming deep purpose has the potential to deliver major gains for both a firm and for society. But it also risks taking a firm out of the frying pan of corporate greed and into the fire of corporate confusion.

The first snapshot in the section outlines the hurdles that firms must overcome in order to dispel the distrust engendered by decades of dissembling about profit-driven business practices. It shows why a primary commitment to customer value is key to getting the benefits of deep purpose – not merely adding some extraneous purpose on top of a profit-obsessed enterprise. Merely "signaling virtue" can distract management from the truly worthwhile goal of co-creating value for customers and can even risk putting the existence of a firm at issue. This article was first published in Forbes.com on February 24, 2022.[78]

At a time of growing distrust of corporations, it is unsurprising to see a rash of books and articles on the moral purpose of a firm. Professor Ranjay Gulati's book, *Deep Purpose: The Heart and Soul of High-Performance Companies* (Penguin, 2022) and the *Harvard Business Review* article "Purposeful Business the Agile Way," by Bain senior partner, Darrell Rigby and colleagues, make key contributions.[79]

5.1.1 The Concept of "Deep Purpose"

Gulati's book introduces the concept of "deep purpose," which has enabled some firms to "operate with heightened passion, urgency, and clarity." It is, writes Gulati, "the missing element behind both exceptional performance and social impact: a perceptible, energizing soul."[80]

Firms with deep purpose have treated "purpose as an existential intention that informed every decision, practice, and process. They adopted purpose as their operating system, perceiving it as a vital animating force with near-spiritual power. As a result, they navigated the tumultuous terrain of multistakeholder capitalism far more adeptly than most, increasing value for all stakeholders, including investors, over the long-term." The word "authentic" occurs forty-four times in the book.

---

[78] S. Denning, "Deep Purpose," *Forbes.com*, February 24, 2022, www.forbes.com/sites/stevedenning/2022/02/24/what-firms-must-learn-about-deep-purpose/.

[79] R. Gulati, *Deep Purpose: The Heart and Soul of High-Performance Companies* (Penguin, 2022); D. Rigby, S. Elk, and S. Berez, "Purposeful Business the Agile Way," *Harvard Business Review*, March 2022, https://hbr.org/2022/03/purposeful-business-the-agile-way.

[80] R. Gulati, *Deep Purpose: The Heart and Soul of High-Performance Companies* (Penguin, 2022), p. 3.

5.1.2 Distinguishing Deep Purpose from Convenient Purpose

A second strength of Gulati's book lies in contrasting deep purpose with "purpose as a tool," "convenient purpose," "shared purpose," and "virtue signaling."
  Gulati writes:

> "Most leaders think of purpose functionally or instrumentally, regarding it as a tool they can wield. Deep purpose leaders think of it as something more fundamental: an existential statement that expresses the firm's very reason for being. Rather than simply pursuing a purpose, these leaders project it faithfully out onto the world. In their hands, purpose serves as an organizing principle that shapes decision-making and binds stakeholders to one another."[81]

Deep Purpose clarifies the meaning of "convenient purpose." Thus, "any number of firms adopt idealistic purpose statements, take a range of actions to serve society, and yet continue to sell products and services that cause serious harm to stakeholders. Depending on your moral perspective, firms that sell fossil fuels, tobacco, alcohol, junk food, weapons, and some social media services all fall into this category."[82] Virtue signaling is very different from deep purpose.

5.1.3 Clarifying the Concept of Deep Purpose

Deep Purpose emphasizes the messiness of decision-making about purpose, which points to the need for clarification of the term.
  Gulati offers a two-part definition. "First, [firms] delineate an ambitious long-term goal for the organization. Second, they give that goal an idealistic cast, committing to the fulfillment of broader social duties."[83]
  This definition has a key gap. If, as the book aspires, the function of deep purpose is to give direction and to serve as an inspiration, deep purpose must be clear enough to provide guidance within the firm as to what *not* to do.

5.1.4 When Purpose Is Unclear, Decision-Making Becomes Confused

The consequence of an unclear purpose is obvious in a case cited by Gulati:

> "Etsy, the online arts-and-crafts marketplace ... founded in 2005 ... [had] always been defined by its purpose of giving 'makers' a venue and tools for marketing their wares and creating their own small businesses. By 2012, under a new CEO ... Etsy had adopted a more ambitious mission – 'to re-imagine commerce in ways that build a more fulfilling and lasting world.'"[84]

---

[81] Ibid., p. 1.   [82] Ibid., p. 4.   [83] Ibid., p. 1.   [84] Ibid., p. 25.

Not surprisingly, with such a vague goal, Etsy lost the plot. Customers were short-changed. Staff benefits mushroomed. Profits declined. The underlying cause? Etsy had adopted a goal that offered no guidance for decision-making. The result? The CEO was fired, and staff cuts were made, as Etsy got back to its primary purpose of co-creating value for customers. With a clear focus on delivering value to its "maker" customers, Etsy is financially back on track, while serving all its stakeholders.

5.1.5 Missing in Action: Co-creating Value for Customers

When capitalism's goal is to make money for the company, it's hardly surprising that firms engage in manipulating, tricking, or even bludgeoning unsuspecting customers into buying things they don't want or need in order to make money for the company. If that is the current purpose of a firm, adding some preachy new social goal on top of that is not going to solve the problem.

However, that is an aberration of the true purpose of a firm. We need to get back to basics and revisit the very purpose of a firm in its core activity. Back in 1954, Peter Drucker had already articulated the goal of customer primacy pithily as "creating a customer." Others expanded this to: "co-creating value for customers."

More recently, Bain senior partner, Darrell Rigby, described the prioritization among stakeholders even more fully:

- "First and foremost, the objective of any business must be to help its customers achieve their goals.
- Second, it is to help employees achieve their full potential ...
- Third, there should be benefits to the communities that the firm serves ...
- Fourth, and finally, a firm must be financially able to maintain operations ...

And ultimately, to survive and thrive in unpredictable environments, companies must do all four things."[85]

The approach here is pragmatic. It aims at expressing the essence of what true capitalism is about and turning squishy philosophical debates into concrete purposeful action.

5.1.6 The Ethics of Customer Capitalism

The idea that creating customers might comprise an inspiring purpose strikes some observers as absurd. As one reader wrote, "In my experience, people need to believe that a company exists for some purpose beyond the

---

[85] S. Denning, "Integrating Agile and Operations," *Forbes.com*, May 22, 2020, www.forbes.com/sites/stevedenning/2020/05/22/how-agile-integrates-operations-and-innovation/.

customer." Moreover, few of the many recent books and articles about corporate purpose cite creating value for customers as being a worthwhile or moral goal.

The culprit here once again is the current aberration of capitalism – maximizing shareholder value as reflected in its stock price. When the firm's only purpose is to make as much money as possible, people are justified in regarding the firm as being involved in something morally dirty. Similarly, when most of the productivity gains created by workers (as shown in Figure 2) are not passed on to those who helped create them and instead are distributed to shareholders and executives, people are right to question whether the core activity of the firm is ethical.[86]

That, however, is the current aberration of capitalism, not the real thing. Customer capitalism is a different animal. Co-creating value for customers is a noble goal. Authentically loving your customer as yourself has deep ethical resonance. Searching for some different or bigger goal risks distraction and failure.

Affirming the deep purpose of delighting customers has vast potential to deliver gains both for a firm and for society. Going beyond this for an even larger goal risks taking a firm out of the frying pan of corporate greed and into the fire of corporate confusion. To achieve the gains while avoiding the risks, leaders need to do more than being authentic. They must master the ten dimensions of corporate purpose, as shown in Figure 18.

Delighting customers is not simply moral. It is also highly pragmatic. The most successful firms today tend to give primacy to the goal of creating value for customers, as shown in Figure 19. That's because, in a marketplace in which power has shifted decisively to customers, delighting customers helps deliver the financial gains that enable the firm to satisfy all the other stakeholders: staff, managers, partners, and shareholders, as well as society at large, as shown in Figure 20.

The financial gains in these firms have been extraordinary. They enable three firms to be in the top twenty firms in terms of attention to the environment.[87] As Apple succinctly expresses it in their vision statement: "we aspire to leave the world better than we found it."

By contrast, firms whose vision and mission are focused on their own success, such as GE, IBM, and GM, as shown in Figure 21, have tended to perform below average in financial terms.

---

[86] S. Denning, "Shift Index," *Forbes.com*, December 15, 2016, www.forbes.com/sites/steveden ning/2016/12/15/shift-index-2016-shows-continuing-decline-in-performance-of-us-firms/.

[87] Y. George, "Top 33 Companies for the Environment," *Forbes.com*, April 22, 2019, www.forbes .com/sites/justcapital/2019/04/22/the-top-33-companies-for-the-environment-by-industry/.

	The ten dimensions of corporate purpose
1.	*The content of the goal:* does the purpose relate to the stakeholders of the firm - customers, managers, staff, partners, society at large, and shareholders, or is it more general outside the firm, for example, "do good?"
2.	*Explicit* vs. *implicit:* Is the goal explicit, or implicit in the firm's actions?
3.	*The clarity of the goal:* Is the goal sufficiently clear to guide staff not only on what to do, but also on what *not* to do?
4.	*Relationship to the firm's behavior.* To what extent is the goal reflected in the firm's behavior?
5.	*Self-interested* vs. *other-directed goals:* Is the goal aimed at benefiting shareholders and its executives or aimed at benefitting customers, users, partners, or society at large?
6.	*Authenticity of C-suite commitment to the goal:* To what extent is the goal deeply and intensely felt by the C-suite as something personally worthwhile, or is it simply a means to another end?
7.	*Authenticity of the staff commitment to the goal:* To what extent is the goal deeply and intensely felt as something personally and authentically worthwhile, or is it simply a means to another end?
8.	*Corporate social responsibility:* To what extent is the goal consistent with and supporting the firm's its corporate and social responsibility?
9.	*Alignment of metrics and rewards alignment with the goal:* To what extent is the firm obsessively measuring performance against the goal and distributing compensation and other rewards accordingly?
10.	*Profitability:* To what extent is the firm achieving satisfactory levels of profitability with a viable business model?

Figure 18 Ten dimensions of corporate purpose

Amazon	VISION: to be Earth's most customer-centric company, where customers can find and discover anything they might want to buy online. MISSION: to offer our customers the lowest possible prices, the best available selection, and the utmost convenience."
Apple	VISION: to make the best products on earth, and to leave the world better than we found it. MISSION: to bring the best personal computing products and support to students, educators, designers, scientists, engineers, businesspersons and consumers in over 140 countries around the world.
Microsoft	VISION: to empower every person and every organization on the planet to achieve more. MISSION: to help people and businesses throughout the world realize their full potential.

Figure 19 Vision/mission statements of Amazon, Apple, and Microsoft
Source: Panmore Institute: http://panmore.com/about

Ten-year total-return increase

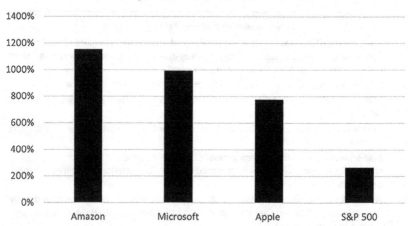

Figure 20 Ten-year total return: Apple, Amazon, Microsoft versus S&P 500[88]

GE	VISION: become the world's premier digital industrial company, transforming industry with software-defined machines and solutions that are connected, responsive, and predictive. MISSION: invent the next industrial era, to build, move, power, and cure the world.
IBM	VISION: to be the world's most successful and important information technology company. MISSION: to lead in the creation, development, and manufacture of the industry's most advanced information technologies, including computer systems, software, networking systems, storage devices, and microelectronics.
GM	VISION: to become the world's most valued automotive company. MISSION: earn customers for life by building brands that inspire passion and loyalty through not only breakthrough technologies but also by serving and improving the communities in which we live and work around the world.

Figure 21 Vision and mission statements: GE, IBM, GM
Source: Panmore Institute: http://panmore.com/about

As shown in Figure 22, the total return of these three firms over ten years is significantly less than the average S&P 500 firm, thus limiting their ability to deliver value to other stakeholders or to society, no matter how deep and authentic their commitment.

---

[88] As of April 21, 2022.

Ten-year total-return change

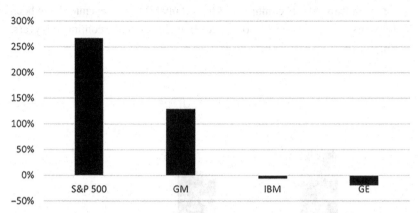

Figure 22 Ten-year total return of GE, IBM, and GM[89]

5.2 How Corporate Purpose Can Signal Virtue but Distract Management

The second snapshot in this chapter shows how embracing a noble social purpose can induce firms to become distracted from their core business, even putting their very existence at stake. The article was first published in Forbes.com on February 23, 2022.[90]

A common flaw of management writing is that it pays insufficient attention to financial performance, and identifies a practice as "a success," without checking to see its financial impact. Nowhere is this more obvious than in management writing about corporate purpose, which often consists of "virtue signaling." This involves citing worthwhile actions in one area to create an aura of virtue over the whole firm, while distracting attention from the more basic issue of the firm's viability.

Take the article, "Use Purpose to Transform Your Workplace" in *Harvard Business Review* about the global firm Unilever.[91] The article describes Unilever's elaborate life-purpose training programs for both employees and gig workers which is aimed at enabling Unilever to "remain true to its mission of making sustainable living commonplace."

One would never guess from the article that Unilever is a firm in significant financial difficulty. Unilever has for many years performed below the average of

---

[89] As of April 21, 2022.

[90] S. Denning, "Corporate Purpose and Signaling Virtue," *Forbes.com*, February 23, 2022, www.forbes.com/sites/stevedenning/2022/02/23/how-corporate-purpose-can-signal-virtue-but-distract-the-management/.

[91] L. Nair, N. Dalton, P. Hull, and W. Kerr, "Use Purpose to Transform Your Workplace," *Harvard Business Review*, March 2022, https://hbr.org/2022/03/use-purpose-to-transform-your-workplace.

firms in the S&P 500, and below that of similar firms in its sector, such as Procter & Gamble (Figure 23).

Even as it trumpets its commitment to sustainability, its revenues have been flat for years, something that is not expected to change in the coming two years. See Figure 24.

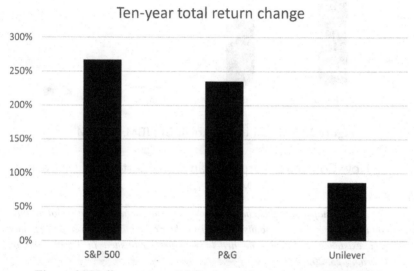

Figure 23 Unilever versus P&G: change in total return 2017–2022

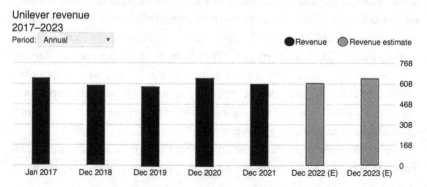

Figure 24 Unilever revenues 2017–2023

5.2.1 Calls for Breakup

Not surprisingly, Unilever's largest shareholders as of February 2022 are calling for a shake-up of the firm, which has 149,000 employees and operates over 400 consumer-goods brands in Asia, Africa, Middle East, Russia, Americas, and Europe. Unilever's global mission is "to do good … together, we can make sustainable living commonplace."

Shareholders are calling for a split into separate divisions for beauty, food, and household products on the grounds that the customer needs in those three sectors are very different. "Talk of synergies between different businesses," said chief investment officer, Bert Flossbach, a top-10 shareholder, "is usually theoretical and designed to keep the status quo, and smaller than the efficiency gains that you would get from a split."[92]

Another top-20 shareholder calls for the removal of the Unilever's chair, and for his replacement from outside the company, to reassess strategy.

In further signs of trouble ahead, it was revealed recently that activist shareholder, Nelson Peltz's investment firm, Trian Partners, had built a stake in Unilever's shareholding and may win a seat on Unilever's board, as he did in his recent engagement with Procter & Gamble. Trian's involvement is a concern for staff who fear more job losses.

Since then, Unilever announced a major reorganization, cutting 1,500 management positions and subdividing the company into five divisions.

5.2.2 Virtue Signaling ahead of Performance

"Public display of climate and social credentials comes at a cost to the business," says fund manager Terry Smith of Fundsmith Equity Fund.[93] "The maker of Dove soap, Hellmann's mayonnaise and Magnum ice cream has set out ambitious climate and social targets and is trying to prove that sustainable business does drive superior financial performance." However, in the absence of that superior financial performance, broader social goals themselves inevitably come into question.

"Unilever seems to be laboring," Smith writes, "under the weight of a management which is obsessed with publicly displaying sustainability credentials at the expense of focusing on the fundamentals of the business."

---

[92] H. Agnew, "Unilever Investors Want Split," *Financial Times*, February 6, 2022, www.ft.com/content/c377abc5-985b-49db-9732-bdaf2483897f.

[93] H. Agnew, "Unilever Has 'Lost the Plot' by fixating on sustainability, says Terry Smith," *Financial Times*, January 11, 2022, www.ft.com/content/7aa44a9a-7fec-4850-8edb-63feee1b837b.

It is not that life-purpose training programs for staff and gig workers are not worthwhile. But their priority within Unilever needs to be viewed in the context of all the other issues facing the firm. When overall performance falls short, broad social goals can become suspects in causing the shortfalls.

Smith adds: "A company which feels it has to define the purpose of Hellmann's mayonnaise has in our view clearly lost the plot. The Hellmann's brand has existed since 1913 so we would guess that by now consumers have figured out its purpose (spoiler alert – salads and sandwiches)."

5.2.3 Digital-Age Management of Mayonnaise

Here, Smith has – perhaps inadvertently – put his finger on a key part of the problem. Unilever is selling a product that your great grandmother used to eat – 1913 mayonnaise – in 2022 and selling it the same way it was sold back then.

In reality, Unilever's mayonnaise comes in multiple modern formats, including the original, extra creamy, light, olive oil, organic spicy chipotle, canola cholesterol-free, and low fat. The problem is that Hellmann's mayonnaise still seen, and marketed, as a hundred-year-old product, not something cool and exciting and adding value to customers.

Thus, there is little, if any, information on the Unilever website about how mayonnaise might enhance customers' lives. There are no innovative recipes or responses to concerns attaching to mayonnaise.

As it happens, Americans have developed a love–hate relationship with mayonnaise. It is the best-selling condiment in North America, but as a high-fat food, mayonnaise is thought by many to be unhealthy. It is mostly oil. It is calorie-rich, and it is easy for the calories to build up. Improperly stored mayonnaise can also be a hotbed for bacteria. In the United States, mayonnaise is made with soy oil, which many nutritionists consider unhealthy, due to its high levels of omega-6 fats. Whether or not these concerns are correct, Unilever needs either to address them or disseminate corrective information.

Unilever needs not only to communicate the answers more effectively but also to build an army of evangelists who carry the brand messages forward. Unless and until management markets mayonnaise as a modern 2022 product, there is little that engaged staff and gig workers can do to help rescue it.

It's about understanding emotional and functional needs of customers at every step along the way, and helping them get toward their goals. The common thread of exponentially growing brands is that they have found an authentic and valuable place in their customers' lives. Unilever needs to find out who its current customers are and discover ways to enrich their lives with its mayonnaise, or find something else that does.

5.2.4 Unilever's Brand versus 400 Product Brands

Mayonnaise is just one of Unilever's 400 products. Each of their products has its own set of issues and opportunities. Obviously, Unilever's top management cannot resolve these issues alone. It needs to be run as a firm that routinely has that capability.

Training gig workers and helping them find their own purpose in life isn't wrong. It could be part of a solution at Unilever. It's just that Unilever has to commit itself first and foremost to adding value to customers' lives, not just waving a public-virtue flag and declaring victory.

6 Fixing the Flaws of the Digital Winners

6.1 Six Lessons That Society Must Learn about Agile

It is a normal part of the competitive flow of capitalism that some firms prosper, while others don't. When some firms grow very rich, very rapidly, the gains that they have made come under special scrutiny, particularly from firms or regions or individuals that have done less well. Questions about whether the winning firms have competed fairly and treated the workers and partners right are of particular concern. As individuals, businesses, communities and even countries are disrupted, tensions can run high. When radically new technology is involved, as with the advent of "the dark satanic mills" of the industrial era, and with the extraordinary technologies of the digital age, suspicions of wrongdoing run rampant.

It is inevitable that regulations designed for very different technology will need to be reviewed and rethought by regulators who may not initially understand what the new technology involves. It is also likely that some of the new corporate titans will overreach in the early days of their success. These tensions are now playing out with the digital winners that have reached global scale at unprecedented speed.

The first snapshot in this section is from 2018. It shows how some flaws need to be addressed by the firms themselves and reinforced by the marketplace. Other flaws may require government intervention. The snapshot explains which is which, and offers six lessons that society must learn about managing the digital economy. In 2018, aggressive regulatory action was still something in the future. This article was first published in Forbes. com on June 27, 2018.[94]

In response to my article, "Why Agile Is Eating the World," which presents Agile as a paradigm shift in management, a reader wrote: "You make a clear case for the amazing progress that Agile discipline has achieved, but also clearly that the winning firms must be regulated. So, is Agile the devil incarnate, or is it our savior? Please clarify on which side of the fence you sit?"[95]

---

[94] S. Denning, "Six Lessons on Agile," *Forbes.com*, June 27, 2018, www.forbes.com/sites/steve denning/2018/06/27/six-lessons-that-society-must-learn-about-agile/.

[95] S. Denning, "Why Agile Is Eating the World," *Forbes.com*, January 2, 2018, www.forbes.com /sites/stevedenning/2018/01/02/why-agile-is-eating-the-world%E2%80%8B%E2%80%8B/? sh=7172c6fa4a5b.

Why Agile is neither panacea nor devil incarnate

Lessons that the marketplace itself will drive

1. Agile innovation is a continuing journey: you never arrive.
2. Avoid sweat-shop workplace.
3. Use Agile to expand into new products and markets.
4. Resist the lure of share buybacks.

Lessons that the public sector may need to reinforce

1. Repeal the 1982 regulation SEC Rule 10b–18
2. Apply anti-trust policy and privacy controls to Silicon Valley

Figure 25 Six lessons society must learn about agile

Let's be clear. I am not suggesting that Agile firms are either saviors or devils. I have yet to see a firm espousing Agile that has no flaws: those flaws must be seen for what they are, and they need to be addressed. If not addressed, they will cause serious financial, economic, or social problems. Some flaws need to be addressed by the firms themselves and will be reinforced by the marketplace. Others may require government intervention, as shown in Figure 25.

6.1.1 Lessons That the Marketplace Itself Will Reinforce

Among the flaws for which the marketplace will by itself tend to generate corrective action are:

Failure to continue innovating: In 2011, Apple innovated by seeing the potential of Siri and incorporating the voice-driven assistant in the iPhone. It was a bold move. Apple had bought Siri from SRI International but then omitted to keep innovating. Siri remained anchored in the menial tasks of finding restaurants and gas stations in the vicinity of the user. Siri's technology could obviously be applied to a much broader array of uses. Apple didn't pursue the possibility. Amazon did. The result? Apple's Siri has been overtaken by Amazon's Alexa, and now Apple is having to play a desperate game of catch-up.

***Lesson*: Agile Innovation Is a Continuing Journey: You Never Arrive**

Sweat-shop workplaces: Agile is a new kind of management that is needed to enable talent to bring their smarts, empathy, and ingenuity to the workplace. Whatever this management is called, it isn't just a new process. It's a fundamentally different way of running an organization. It is more productive for the company. And it has immense potential benefit for the human spirit by encouraging the talent to "love their customers as themselves." It can create workplaces that enable human beings to do something worthwhile and meaningful – co-creating value for other human beings. The end of wage-slavery in the workplace is a big deal on multiple fronts, provided that the firm plays the game this way.

Some firms, however, have imposed sweat-shop conditions for at least parts of their firm in a way that is antithetical to the spirit of Agile management. Such practices lead inexorably to a reversion to bureaucratic command-and-control and loss of the benefits of a highly motivated workforce. This reversion will in due course create a negative reputation for the firm and make it difficult to recruit talent in future. If not resolved, it will hinder the long-term growth and the eventual survival of the firm.

Lesson: Avoid Sweat-Shop Workplaces

Short-termism: Some firms embrace Agile management while trying to comply with stock market pressures for increases in quarterly earnings. This can come at the expense of long-term investments in research and development and expanding into new products and new markets. The pressure for short-term results can jeopardize long-term growth. Any shortfalls in earnings can then create increased pressure on the stock to cut costs, which further prevents the firm from taking steps to create long-term value. As the major financial gains of Agile are likely to come from market-creating innovations which draw in new customers, the long-term success of the firm will depend on such innovations.

Lesson: Use Agile to Expand into New Products and Markets

Share buybacks: *The Economist* has condemned them.[96] *The Financial Times* has denounced them.[97] A *Harvard Business Review* article has called them "stock price manipulation."[98] These influential journals make a powerful case that wholesale stock buybacks are a bad idea – bad economically, bad financially, bad socially, bad legally, and bad morally. There is growing recognition, even on Wall Street, that share buybacks don't work even on their own terms.

Lesson: Resist the lure of share buybacks

---

[96] S. Denning, "The Economist: Blue-Chips Are Addicted to 'Corporate Cocaine'," *Forbes.com*, September 19, 2014, www.forbes.com/sites/stevedenning/2014/09/19/the-economist-blue-chips-are-addicted-to-corporate-cocaine/.

[97] D. McCrum, "The Case against Share Buybacks," *Financial Times*, January 30, 2018, www.ft .com/content/e7fb2144-fbae-11e7-a492-2c9be7f3120a.

[98] W. Lazonick, "Profits without Prosperity," *Harvard Business Review*, September 2014, https:// hbr.org/2014/09/profits-without-prosperity.

6.1.2 Lessons That the Public Sector May Need to Enforce

The flaws that the marketplace will not by itself correct include the following:

Rethink maximizing shareholder value: Some firms try to combine Agile management with the goal of maximizing value for shareholder as the sole purpose of a corporation. This goal, which, as Steven Pearlstein pointed out, "is now taught in every business school, repeated in every earnings call and annual report and waved around by every activist investor, has no basis in law or logic or any credible theory of how a company should be managed."[99]

Nevertheless, the goal of maximizing shareholder value is now so deeply entrenched in US public corporations, and supported by massive share buybacks that hide the lack of long-term growth strategies, it seems likely that it will continue unless and until there is either a major global financial crash or the repeal of Rule 10-18b – the 1982 SEC regulation which exempts open-market stock buybacks from the obvious charge of stock price manipulation and self-dealing.

Lesson: Repeal the 1982 SEC Rule 10b-18

Abuse of monopoly power and privacy: Because Agile firms like Apple, Amazon, Facebook, and Google are so successful, there are temptations for them to use their market power in negative ways.[100] Thus, the successful exponents of Agile are becoming so dominant in the marketplace that they are now emerging as a threat to a free society, in the much same way, *mutatis mutandis*, that the big industrial companies of the late nineteenth Century (rail, oil, steel) became a threat to society. That's a job for the public sector.

True, it's hard to see how all this will happen in the current political environment. But it has to happen, if a free society is to survive. Monopolies have always been, and will always be, a potential evil. If not regulated, they will destroy the capitalist system that created them. We have seen this movie before, many times. Silicon Valley has been given a free pass from public scrutiny for a long time. We know how to fix these things. What we need is the willpower to do it.

Lesson: Evolve Anti-Trust Policy and Privacy Controls to Cover Digital

Thus, we need to see Agile and the digital economy by the clear light of day, neither through rose-colored spectacles in which everything is kumbaya, nor

---

[99] S. Pearstein, "Five Myths about Capitalism," *The Washington Post*, September 27, 2018, www.washingtonpost.com/outlook/five-myths/five-myths-about-capitalism/2018/09/27/3f0b72f6-c06f-11e8-90c9-23f963eea204_story.html.

[100] D. Dayen, "Big Tech: The New Predatory Capitalism," *American Prospect*, Winter 2018, https://issuu.com/americanprospect/docs/tap_winter_2018.

through a glass darkly in which everything is evil. The saying "you can't have it both ways" doesn't mean that we can't walk and chew gum at the same time.

6.2 Why Big Tech Should Regulate Itself

The second snapshot in this section comes from 2020, when the public mood was much more negative and aggressive than in 2018. The snapshot examines the contagious narrative that most of the ills of society derive from the missteps of Big Tech. A US Congressional hearing in 2020 revealed the intensity of the bipartisan venom against these firms and the efforts to rein them in or even hamstring them.

At the same time, the obfuscations of some of the CEOs appearing before Congress did their own cause little good. The hearing pointed to the need for the firms themselves to do a better job of presenting their own case to the public, while also paying more attention to regulating themselves.

Now in 2022, a Democratic administration has appointed key people to tackle the regulatory issues of Big Tech, but it is unclear what if any action will be taken, given the distractions of the COVID-19 pandemic, the war in Ukraine, and a wave of inflation.[101] This article was published in Forbes.com on August 2, 2020.[102]

It was hard to recall last week, as Google's CEO Sundar Pichai answered repeated accusations by a Congressional Antitrust Subcommittee of dubious conduct, that Google once proudly embraced a code of conduct in which "Don't be evil" and "acting honorably" were front and center. Around April 2018, Google's code of conduct was changed to reflect a vaguer commitment to "do the right thing" while merely "measuring themselves against the highest possible standards of ethical business conduct," that is, in effect, business as usual.[103]

Last week, the Antitrust Subcommittee had summoned the chief executives of Amazon, Apple, Facebook and Alphabet (Google) to grill them on how their companies maintain, enhance or abuse their quasi-monopoly power. In the six-hour session, members cross-examined the CEOs on alleged misstep after misstep, often not waiting for a response to their demands for yes/no answers. In addition to the announced topic of antitrust violations, members also diverged into other issues of abuse of privacy, political bias, and conspiracy theories.

---

[101] S. Kolhatkar, "Lina Khan & Big Tech," *New Yorker*, December 12, 2021, www.newyorker.com/magazine/2021/12/06/lina-khans-battle-to-rein-in-big-tech.

[102] S. Denning, "Why Big Tech Should Regulate Itself," *Forbes.com*, August 2, 2020, www.forbes.com/sites/stevedenning/2020/08/02/why-big-tech-should-regulate-itself/.

[103] Montti, R. "Google's 'Don't Be Evil' No Longer Prefaces Code of Conduct" SEJ, May 20, 2018, https://www.searchenginejournal.com/google-dont-be-evil/254019/.

6.2.1 A Wake-Up Call for the Big Four

The session should be a wake-up call for the CEOs of firms that have long bathed in the positive glow from the vast array of benefits that they have showered on users and customers and the unprecedented market capitalizations that Wall Street has bestowed on them. In earlier years, they had also benefited from the notion that Silicon Valley companies were somehow different from big business with their easy-going California lifestyle and staff benefits, like free food and games. Yet the four firms are now bigger than big. Together with Microsoft, they are valued at more than $6 trillion, equivalent to more than a quarter of the entire US economy – far bigger than the industrial giants of the twentieth century.

What was striking was the unanimous animosity towards the four. Both Democrats and Republicans argued relentlessly that the four – Amazon, Apple, Facebook and Google – were all doing bad things. The hearing showed that these firms are now facing brutal political scrutiny.

6.2.2 Diverging Preparedness

The preparedness of the lawmakers was also striking. The members had done their homework and were engaged in a coordinated set of attacks, no holds barred. Each member had selected a particular area to probe and was ready with detailed examples, with question after question, often not staying for a detailed answer, interrupting the CEO's explanation with a statement, "I will take that to be a yes, and we need to move on."

By comparison, the CEOs seemed unprepared for the venom. They presented themselves as being unable to recall some of the most famous cases (e.g., Jeff Bezos on Amazon's involvement with diapers[104]). They said they could not remember even recent Wall Street Journal articles about their supposed wrongdoing.[105] They promised to "get back to the committee." Tactically, that looked as though they were counting on lobbying and the Senate to block any change.

The tech titans no doubt sought to avoid appearing contentious. While never actually admitting wrongdoing, Amazon's Jeff Bezos said that he couldn't guarantee that wrongdoing had never happened and assured the committee that he was looking into it. By feigning ignorance, the CEOs at least postponed the day of reckoning.

---

[104] W. Oremus, "How Bezos Went Thermonuclear on Diapers," *Slate*, October 2013, https://slate.com/technology/2013/10/amazon-book-how-jeff-bezos-went-thermonuclear-on-diapers-com.html.

[105] Ibid.

The CEOs also tried to get by with the usual subterfuges, such as "You are in control of your data," "You have lots of choice," "We're not really that big," "We provide relevant information," and "We are apolitical," even as the members continued to poke gaping holes in these half-truths.[106]

Perhaps the CEOs were not expecting the preparedness or virulence of the attacks. They could have been lulled into nonchalance by the extraordinary financial gains that they were about to announce the following day. These extraordinary profits and unprecedented market capitalizations reflect the fact that digital technologies have enabled workers to do their jobs from home, students to continue their classes while schools are closed, and people to stay in touch with loved ones and entertain themselves while sheltering in place. Tech companies have been reaping enormous benefits from this shift. In essence, through Agile management and network effects, these firms reliably deliver benefits to customers and customers love the benefits they receive. Bezos noted that trust in Amazon is around 80%, while refraining from mentioning that trust in Congress is less than 20%.

6.2.3 The Failure to Make an Antitrust Case

Despite their preparation, the lawmakers failed to come to grips with the antitrust issue. Antitrust law is currently based on damage to customers. Few, if any, of the many examples showed damage to customers. They were almost all about damage to other businesses and possible competitors. So, on a strict legal basis, the case for wrongdoing on current antitrust law was never made.

The Democratic members cited example after example where other businesses were being hurt, including those businesses that had signed on Amazon's platform as potential partners. Implicitly, the lawmakers were making an argument for changing the antitrust law.

6.2.4 A Change in Antitrust Law

It will, however, be tricky to come up with a definition of "unfair competition," given that the very driver of capitalism is competition. What is needed, according to columnist Steven Pearlstein is a major rewrite of the industrial-era antitrust statutes.[107] That's because current antitrust doctrines are too limited to adequately protect competition or stop anticompetitive conduct. A rewrite is

---

[106] G. Fowler, "Big Tech CEO Hearing Lies," *The Washington Post*, July 29, 2020, www .washingtonpost.com/technology/2020/07/29/big-tech-ceo-hearing-lies/.

[107] S. Pearlstein, "Beating up on Big Tech is Fun and Easy. Restraining It Will Require Rewriting the Law," *The Washington Post*, July 30, 2020, www.washingtonpost.com/business/2020/07/ 30/antitrust-amazon-apple-facebook-google/.

needed to prevent "over-consolidation in virtually every sector of the economy, nowhere more so than in tech … "

According to Bill Baer, who headed the Justice Department's antitrust division during the Obama administration, "We went from an antitrust culture [in the 1970s] where 'the government always wins' to one where enforcers almost always lost, or where fear of losing caused the government not to act at all."[108]

Pearlstein makes the case for a twenty-first century antitrust law that would "protect and enhance competition not only because it lowers prices, increases choice and improves quality for consumers, but also because it stimulates innovation, reduces income inequality and reduces the concentration of economic and political power."

"This would not be the first time," writes Pearlstein, "that Congress has had to step in to revive and update the antitrust law – it happened in 1914, 1936, 1950 and 1976."

6.2.5 The Problem with Big Tech

There is thus a growing political and analytic consensus that these firms present a substantive problem. They grew very big because of digital management and network effects that ended up conferring huge benefits on customers and the firms themselves. Now they are de facto monopolies and like all monopolies they have started doing questionable things.

The wrongdoing has taken an aggravated form, given that these firms have become so dominant that they have become in effect utilities. There are some behaviors that would be acceptable if they were just one path among many, but not acceptable when they have become in effect the main public highway.

6.2.6 The Options for Big Tech

Big Tech has two main options. They can go on acting as if nothing is amiss and hope that government action will take a long time to become a reality. Or they can take proactive steps to recognize the legitimacy of the issues and regulate themselves with a commitment to reengage with "acting honorably" and "doing no evil." The latter course of action will be smarter and less painful.

We have seen this movie before. In 2001, an American antitrust law case accused Microsoft of illegally maintaining its monopoly position in the PC market. The case was eventually settled but the result was almost the same as if Microsoft had lost. Lawyers started appearing in every internal meeting in

---

[108] Ibid.

Microsoft, raising questions about how any statement or decision would look in an antitrust hearing. It took more than a decade for Microsoft to recover its entrepreneurial spirit.

Microsoft was notable for its absence from the 2020 Congressional hearing. Microsoft has learned that moderating its own conduct is preferable to attempting to extract the last drop of profit in a world in which they are already swimming in unprecedented profits.

Google had it right the first time, when it proudly embraced a code of conduct in which "don't be evil" and "acting honorably" were front and center. The Big Four have grown big by creating great workplaces that ended up conferring benefits on customers. Now they need to raise their sights and take a further step: do the right thing by society by not abusing their market power.

Regulation is coming: the only question is whether the big four will do it themselves or have it done to them.

7 Shareholder Capitalism

7.1 The Origin of the World's Dumbest Idea: Milton Friedman

This section describes the aberrant form of capitalism – maximizing shareholder value as reflected in the current stock price (MSV) – a theory that has dominated the management of public companies, particularly in the United States, for the last half-century.

The first snapshot shows how the idea of MSV emerged from the work of the Nobel-Prize-winning economist Milton Friedman, and his economist colleagues, Michael Jensen and William Meckling.[109] It explains why MSV turned out to be the disease of which it purported to be the cure. This article was published in Forbes. com on June 25, 2013.[110]

No popular idea ever has a single origin. But the idea that the sole purpose of a firm is to make money for its shareholders got going in a major way with an article by Milton Friedman in *The New York Times* on September 13, 1970.

As the leader of the Chicago school of economics, and the winner of the Nobel Prize in Economics in 1976, Friedman has been described by *The Economist* as "the most influential economist of the second half of the 20th century." The impact of the *New York Times* article led to columnist George Will's salute to Friedman as "the most consequential public intellectual of the 20th century."[111] And indeed, Friedman did come to represent the spirit of capitalism for the next half century."

Friedman's article was ferocious in its love of money. Any business executives who pursued a goal other than making money were, he said, "unwitting puppets of the intellectual forces that have been undermining the basis of a free society these past decades." They were guilty of "analytical looseness and lack of rigor." They had even turned themselves into "unelected government officials" who were illegally taxing employers and customers.

How did the Nobel-prize winner arrive at these conclusions? It's curious that a paper which accuses others of "analytical looseness and lack of rigor" assumes its conclusion before it begins. "In a free-enterprise, private-property system," the article states at the outset as an obvious truth requiring no justification or

---

[109] S. Denning, "The Dumbest Idea in the World: Maximizing Shareholder Value." *Forbes.com*, November 28, 2011," www.forbes.com/sites/stevedenning/2011/11/28/maximizing-shareholder-value-the-dumbest-idea-in-the-world/.

[110] S. Denning, "Origin of the World's Dumbest Idea," *Forbes.com*, June 26, 2013, www .forbes.com/sites/stevedenning/2013/06/26/the-origin-of-the-worlds-dumbest-idea-milton-friedman/.

[111] G. F. Will, "Many of the Century," *Hoover Digest*, October 30, 2002, www.hoover.org/research/man-century (reprinted from *The Washington Post*).

proof, "a corporate executive is an employee of the owners of the business," namely, the shareholders.

Come again?

It is a rudimentary legal truth that a corporate executive is not an employee of the shareholders. An executive is an employee of the corporation.

7.1.1 An Organization Is a Mere Legal Fiction

But in the magical world conjured up in this article, an organization is a mere "legal fiction," which Friedman simply ignores to prove the predetermined conclusion. The executive "has direct responsibility to his employers." that is, the shareholders. "That responsibility is to conduct the business in accordance with their desires, which generally will be to make as much money as possible while conforming to the basic rules of the society, both those embodied in law and those embodied in ethical custom."

What's interesting is that, while the article jettisons one legal reality – the corporation – as a mere legal fiction, it rests its entire argument on another legal reality – the law of agency – as the foundation for its conclusions. The article thus picks and chooses which parts of legal reality are mere "legal fictions" to be ignored and which parts are "rock-solid foundations" for public policy. The choice depends on the predetermined conclusion to be proved.

A corporate executive who devotes any money for any general social interest would, the article says, "be spending someone else's money ... Insofar as his actions in accord with his 'social responsibility' reduce returns to stockholders, he is spending their money."

How did the corporation's money somehow become the shareholder's money? Simple. That is the article's starting assumption. By assuming away the existence of the corporation as a mere "legal fiction," hey presto! the corporation's money magically becomes the stockholders' money.

But the conceptual sleight of hand doesn't stop there. The article goes on: "Insofar as his actions raise the price to customers, he is spending the customers' money." One moment ago, the organization's money was the stockholder's money. But suddenly in this phantasmagorical world, the organization's money has become the customer's money. With another wave of Professor Friedman's conceptual wand, the customers have acquired a notional "right" to a product at a certain price and any money over and above that price has magically become "theirs."

But even then, the intellectual fantasy isn't finished. The article continues: "Insofar as [the executives'] actions lower the wages of some employees; he is spending their money." Now suddenly, the organization's money has become, not the stockholder's money or the customers' money, but the employees' money.

Is the money the stockholders', the customers', or the employees'? Apparently, it can be any of those possibilities, depending on which argument Friedman is trying to make. In Friedman's wondrous world, the money is anyone's except that of the real legal owner of the money: the corporation.

One might think that such nonsense would have been quickly spotted and denounced as absurd. And it was. Professor Joseph L. Bower, then a young associate professor at Harvard Business School, was interviewed by National Public Radio and declared that maximizing shareholder value as the sole goal of business was "pernicious nonsense."

And perhaps if the article had been written by someone other than the leader of the Chicago school of economics and a front-runner for the Nobel Prize in Economics that was to come in 1976, the article would have been ignored. But instead, this magical fantasy obtained widespread support as the new gospel of business.

7.1.2 People Just Wanted to Believe

The success of the article was not because the arguments were sound or powerful, but rather because businessmen desperately *wanted* to believe. At the time, private sector firms were starting to feel the pressures of global competition and executives were looking around for ways to increase their returns. The idea of focusing totally on making money, and forgetting about any concerns for employees, customers or society was an avenue worth exploring, regardless of the argumentation.

In fact, the argument was so attractive that, six years later, it was dressed up in fancy mathematics to become one of the most famous and widely cited academic business articles of all time. In 1976, Finance professor Michael Jensen and Dean William Meckling of the Simon School of Business at the University of Rochester published their paper in the *Journal of Financial Economics* entitled "Theory of the Firm: Managerial Behavior, Agency Costs and Ownership Structure."

Underneath impenetrable jargon and abstruse mathematics is the reality that the intellectual edifice of the famous article rests on the same false assumption as Professor Friedman's article, namely, that an organization is a legal fiction which doesn't exist, and that the organization's money is owned by the stockholders.

Even better for executives, the article proposed that, to ensure that the firms would focus solely on making money for the shareholders, firms should turn their executives into major shareholders, by affording them generous compensation in the form of stock. In this way, the alleged tendency of executives to feather their own nests would be encouraged and mobilized in the interests of the shareholders.

7.1.3 The Money Took Over

Sadly, as often happens with bad ideas that make some people rich, MSV caught on and became the conventional wisdom. Not surprisingly, executives were only too happy to accept the generous stock compensation being offered. In due course, they even came to view it as an entitlement, independent of performance.

Politics also lent support. Ronald Reagan was elected in the United States in 1980 with his message that government is "the problem." In the United Kingdom, Margaret Thatcher became Prime Minister in 1979. These leaders preached "economic freedom" and urged a focus on making money as "the solution." As the Gordon Gekko character in the 1987 movie, *Wall Street*, pithily summarized the philosophy, greed was now good.

7.1.4 Paying Bureaucrats like Entrepreneurs

Bower points to the 1990 article in *Harvard Business Review* by Michael Jensen and Kevin Murphy, which put shareholder value thinking on steroids. The article, "CEO Incentives – It's Not How Much You Pay, but How," suggested that CEOs were being paid like bureaucrats and that this caused them to act like bureaucrats. "Is it any wonder," Jensen and Murphy wrote, "that so many CEOs act like bureaucrats rather than the value-maximizing entrepreneurs that companies need to enhance their standing in world markets?" Instead, they should be paid with significant amounts of stock so that their interests would be aligned with stockholders.[112]

"That article," Bower told me recently, "was very well received on Wall Street. They loved it. You could see the change in compensation practices. The use of the phrase 'maximize shareholder value' exploded at that time."

And indeed, CEOs became very entrepreneurial – but in *their own cause,* not necessarily the organization's. The impact on CEO compensation practices was mind-boggling. Even as real organizational performance in terms of the rates of return on assets has been drastically declining, studies by professors Lazonick and Hopkins show that in the period 1978 to 2013, CEO compensation increased by an astonishing 937%, while the typical worker's compensation grew by a meager 10%.[113]

The preference for capital over labor has been a characteristic of capitalism from its outset. In the last fifty years, however, that preference shifted from the long-term prospects of the firm and its shareholders to the narrower focus of the

---

[112] M. Jensen, "CEO Incentives: Not How Much but How," *Harvard Business Review*, May 1990, https://hbr.org/1990/05/ceo-incentives-its-not-how-much-you-pay-but-how.

[113] W. Lazonick and M. Hopkins, "Comment on the SEC Pay Ratio Disclosure Rule," *U.S. Securities and Exchange Commission*, March 21, 2017, www.sec.gov/comments/pay-ratio-statement/cll3-1658300-148764.pdf.

current stock price. This shift transformed the relationships between capital and labor, in favor of capital, and moved the management focus to extracting short-term gain. Accordingly, the inequalities of capitalism, and the problem of short-termism, were gravely aggravated.

Customer benefits also increased enormously in the same period, but when executives treat themselves so richly, and those creating the customer value are treated so poorly, it is not surprising that there is socially explosive inequality and bipartisan demands in congress for basic change.

7.1.5 Business Roundtable 1997

In 1997, it became official. In a formal statement, the Business Roundtable declared its wish

> to emphasize that the principal objective of a business enterprise is to gener-
> ate economic returns to its owners . . . . if the CEO and the directors are not
> focused on stockholder value, it may be less likely the corporation will realize
> that value . . . the paramount duty of management and of boards of directors is
> to the corporation's stockholders; the interests of other stakeholders are
> relevant as a derivative of the duty to stockholders.

The Business Roundtable also rejected stakeholder capitalism. "The notion that the board must somehow balance the interests of stockholders against the interests of other stakeholders fundamentally misconstrues the role of directors. It is, moreover, an unworkable notion because it would leave the board with no criterion for resolving conflicts between interests of stockholders and of other stakeholders or among different groups of stakeholders."[114] In this way, MSV became the official business policy of the United States. Self-interest was to reign supreme, from the board on down.

The ethics of the approach were illustrated by the perversely enlightening book, *Hardball* (2004), by George Stalk, Jr. and Rob Lachenauer. Firms, they said, should aggressively pursue shareholder value to win in the marketplace. Firms should be "willing to hurt their rivals." They should be "ruthless" and "mean." Exponents of the approach should "enjoy watching their competitors squirm." In an effort to win, they should go to the very edge of illegality or if they go over the line, get off with civil penalties that appear large in absolute terms but meager in relation to the illicit gains that are made.

Amid such avaricious thinking, it was hardly surprising, as Roger Martin wrote in his book, *Fixing the Game*, that the corporate world is plagued by continuing scandals, such as the accounting scandals in 2001–2002 with Enron,

---

[114] ""Statement on Corporate Governance," *Business Roundtable*, September 1997.

WorldCom, Tyco International, Global Crossing, and Adelphia, the options backdating scandals of 2005–2006, and the subprime meltdown of 2007–2008. Banks and others have been gaming the system, first with practices that were shady but not strictly illegal and then with practices that were criminal. They included insider trading, price fixing of LIBOR, abuses in foreclosure, money laundering for drug dealers and terrorists, assisting tax evasion and misleading clients with worthless securities.

Martin writes:

> "It isn't just about the money for shareholders, or even the dubious CEO behavior that our theories encourage. It's much bigger than that. Our theories of shareholder value maximization and stock-based compensation have the ability to destroy our economy and rot out the core of American capitalism. These theories underpin regulatory fixes instituted after each market bubble and crash. Because the fixes begin from the wrong premise, they will be ineffectual; until we change the theories, future crashes are inevitable."

7.1.6 Jack Welch: "The Dumbest Idea in The World"

In 2009, a former champion of shareholder value thinking reemerged as a strident critic: Jack Welch. During his tenure as CEO of GE from 1981 to 2001, Jack Welch came to be seen as the outstanding implementer of MSV, given his capacity to grow shareholder value and hit his numbers almost exactly, with his agenda of downsizing, deal-making, and financialization.[115] When Jack Welch retired, the company had gone from a market value of $14 billion to $484 billion at the time of his retirement, making it, according to the stock market, the most valuable and largest company in the world. In 1999, he was named "Manager of the Century" by *Fortune* magazine.[116]

In the years since Jack Welch retired from GE in 2001, GE's stock price has not fared well: in the decade following Welch's departure, GE lost around 60 percent of the market capitalization that Welch had "created." It turned out that the fabulous returns of GE during the Welch era were obtained in part by the risky financial leverage of GE Capital, which would have collapsed in 2008 if it had not been for a government bailout.

In due course, Jack Welch became a forceful opponent of shareholder value theory. On March 12, 2009, in an interview with the *Financial Times*, he said,

---

[115] S. Denning, "Why Jack Welch Failed to Break Capitalism," *Forbes.com*, June 12, 2022, www .forbes.com/sites/stevedenning/2022/06/12/why-jack-welch-failed-to-break-capitalism/.

[116] G. Colvin, "The Manager of the Century," *Fortune*, November 22, 1999, https://archive .fortune.com/magazines/fortune/fortune_archive/1999/11/22/269126/index.htm.

"On the face of it, shareholder value is the dumbest idea in the world. Shareholder value is a result, not a strategy ... your main constituencies are your employees, your customers and your products. Managers and investors should not set share price increases as their overarching goal ... Short-term profits should be allied with an increase in the long-term value of a company."[117]

7.1.7 Share Buybacks

In 2014, business professor William Lazonick presented the business world with even more astonishing news: many major public corporations were engaged in buying back their own shares to an extent that constituted illegal stock price manipulation on a macroeconomic scale.[118] Mainstream journals picked up the theme. *The Economist* called share buybacks "an addiction to corporate cocaine." Reuters called it "self-cannibalization." *The Financial Times* called it "an overwhelming conflict of interest." In March 2015, Lazonick's article won the *HBR* McKinsey Award for the best *HBR* article of the year.[119]

How had so many of the biggest and most respected companies in the world gotten involved in illegal stock price manipulation on such a vast scale? Why is it still tolerated by regulators? It's simple, Lazonick explains. Once firms began in the 1980s to focus on maximizing shareholder value as reflected in the current share price, the actual capacity of these firms to generate real value for the organization and their shareholders began to decline, as cost-cutting, dispirited staff, and limited capacity to innovate took their toll. The C-suite faced a dilemma. They had promised increasing shareholder value, and yet their actions were systematically destroying the capacity to create that value. What to do?

They hit upon a wondrous shortcut: why bother to *create* new value for shareholders? Why not simply *extract* value that the organization had already accumulated and transfer it directly to the shareholders (including themselves) by way of buying back their own shares? By reducing the number of shares,

---

[117] F. Guerra, "Welch Condemns Share Price Focus," *Financial Times*, March 12, 2009, www .ft.com/content/294ff1f2-0f27-11de-ba10-0000779fd2ac.

[118] W. Lazonick, "Profits without Prosperity," *Harvard Business Review*, September 2014, https:// hbr.org/2014/09/profits-without-prosperity.

[119] S. Denning, "The Economist, Blue Chips Are Addicted to Corporate Cocaine," *Forbes.com*, April 19, 2014, www.forbes.com/sites/stevedenning/2014/09/19/the-economist-blue-chips-are-addicted-to-corporate-cocaine/; K. Brettell, D. Gaffen and D. Rohde, "The Cannibalized Company: How the Cult of Shareholder Value Has Reshaped Corporate America; A Special Report," *Reuters*, November 16, 2015, www.reuters.com/investigates/special-report/usa-buybacks-cannibalized; J. Plender, "Blowing the Whistle on Buybacks and Value Destruction," *Financial Times*, March 1, 2016, www.ft.com/content/0b71ca32-df0b-11e5-b67f-a61732c1d025; S. Denning, "The Best Management Article of 2014," *Forbes.com*, March 26, 2015, www .forbes.com/sites/stevedenning/2015/03/26/the-best-management-article-of-2014/.

firms could boost their earnings per share. The result was usually a short-term bump in the stock price – and short-term shareholder value.

There was just one snag. Jacking up the share price with share buybacks would constitute stock price manipulation and hence would be illegal. But no problem! In 1982, the Reagan administration was happy to remove the impediment and the SEC instituted Rule 10b-18 of the Securities Exchange Act.

Naturally, the SEC didn't announce that stock-price manipulation was being legalized. That would have created a political outcry. Instead, they passed a complicated rule that made it seem that stock price manipulation was still illegal, but provided protection to firms so that it would almost invulnerable to legal challenge.

And so, the floodgates opened. The resulting scale of share buybacks is mind-boggling. Over the years 2006–2015, the 459 companies in the S&P 500 Index that were publicly listed over the ten-year period expended $3.9 trillion on share buybacks, representing 54% of net income, in addition to another 37% of net income on dividends.

7.1.8 The Disastrous Consequences

Once these financial tricks were understood, the underlying reality became apparent. The decline that Friedman and other sensed in 1970 turned out to be real and persistent. The rate of return on assets and on invested capital of US firms declined from 1965 to 2009 by three-quarters, as shown by the Shift Index, a study of 20,000 US firms.[120]

The shareholder value theory thus failed even on its own narrow terms: making money. The proponents of shareholder value and stock-based executive compensation hoped that their theories would focus executives on improving the real performance of their companies and thus increasing shareholder value over time. Yet precisely the opposite occurred. In the period of shareholder capitalism since 1976, executive compensation exploded while corporate performance declined.

7.1.9 The Disease of Which It Purported to Be the Cure

As Roger Martin in his book, *Fixing the Game*, noted,

> "between 1960 and 1980, CEO compensation per dollar of net income earned for
> the 365 biggest publicly traded American companies fell by 33 percent. CEOs
> earned more for their shareholders for steadily less and less relative

---

[120] S. Denning, "Shift Index," *Forbes.com*, December 15, 2016, www.forbes.com/sites/steveden ning/2016/12/15/shift-index-2016-shows-continuing-decline-in-performance-of-us-firms/.

compensation. By contrast, in the decade from 1980 to 1990, CEO compensation per dollar of net earnings produced *doubled*. From 1990 to 2000 it quadrupled."

In effect, maximizing shareholder value as reflected in the current stock price is not just obsolete. It is financially, economically, socially, and morally wrong. Yet there are powerful vested interests in keeping things as they are. As Upton Sinclair pointed out a century ago, "It's hard to get a man to understand something when he is being paid not to understand it."

7.2 Is Maximizing Shareholder Value Finally Dying?

The second snapshot in this section is an article published in Forbes.com on August 19, 2019 – the day on which the Business Roundtable reversed its support for MSV and declared that firms should create value to all the stakeholders.[121] The article concludes that shareholder value thinking continues even today, behind a façade of stakeholder capitalism.[122]

It's a big news day for big-business watchers. It's as if a hurricane had struck Wall Street:

- "Shareholder Value Is No Longer Everything, Top CEOs Say" is the lead story in *The New York Times*.[123]
- "CEO Group Says Maximizing Shareholder Profits Can't Be Main Goal" is the top story in *The Washington Post*.[124]
- "Group of US Corporate Leaders Ditches Shareholder-First Mantra" declares the front page of the *Financial Times*.[125]
- "Move Over, Shareholders: Top CEOs Say Companies Have Obligations to Society" states the front page of *The Wall Street Journal*.[126]

---

[121] S. Denning, "Why the World's Dumbest Idea Is Dying," *Forbes.com*, August 19, 2019, www .forbes.com/sites/stevedenning/2019/08/19/why-maximizing-shareholder-value-is-finally-dying/.

[122] S. Denning, "Why Maximizing Shareholder Value Is Finally Dying" *Forbes.com*, August 19, 2019, www.forbes.com/sites/stevedenning/2019/08/19/why-maximizing-shareholder-value-is-finally-dying/.

[123] D. Gelles and D. Yaffe-Bellany, "Shareholder Value Is No Longer Everything, Top C.E.O.s Say," *The New York Times*, August 19, 2019, www.nytimes.com/2019/08/19/business/business-roundtable-ceos-corporations.html.

[124] S. Pearlstein, "Top CEOs are Reclaiming Legitimacy by Advancing a Vision of What's Good for America," *The Washington Post*, August 19, 2019, www.washingtonpost.com/business/2019/08/19/top-ceos-are-reclaiming-legitimacy-by-advancing-vision-whats-good-america/.

[125] R. Henderson and P. Temple, "Group of US Corporate Leaders Ditches Shareholder-First Mantra," *Financial Times*, August 19, 2019, www.ft.com/content/e21a9fac-c1f5-11e9-a8e9 -296ca66511c9.

[126] D. Benoit, "Move Over, Shareholders: Top CEOs Say Companies Have Obligations to Society," *Wall Street Journal*, August 19, 2019, www.wsj.com/articles/business-roundtable-steps-back-from-milton-friedman-theory-11566205200.

The hubbub concerns today's declaration by the BRT that profits for share-holders are no longer the only purpose of a corporation. This is a big deal. For the last two decades, this group of some 200 powerful CEOs had stuck to the mantra, "maximize shareholder value," and most of its members had faithfully implemented it. Now official cover for MSV is gone. The question remains to what goals its members will now pursue.

7.2.1 Maximizing Shareholder Value

The BRT has a long track record of defending business against the wider interests of society. In 1975, it helped defeat anti-trust legislation. In 1977, it helped block a plan for a consumer protection agency and helped stymie labor law reform. In 1985, it won a reduction in corporate taxes. And in 1997, it issued its policy statement to the effect that "the principal objective of a business enterprise is to generate returns for its owners."[127]

While the notion of shareholder value is valid to the extent that corporations do need to deliver value to shareholders over the long term, the shareholder value doctrine had come to mean something quite different in practice, particu-larly in US business.

As analyst Steven Pearlstein explains in *The Washington Post*: "In its more corrosive application – the one inculcated in business schools, enforced by corporate lawyers, and demanded by activist investors and Wall Street analysts – maximizing shareholder value has meant doing whatever is necessary to boost the share price this quarter and the next."

"Over the years, it has been used to justify bamboozling customers, squeez-ing workers and suppliers, avoiding taxes and lavishing stock options on executives. Most of what people find so distasteful about American capitalism – the ruthlessness, the greed, the inequality – has its roots in this misguided notion about what business is all about."[128]

The result? By 2019, maximizing shareholder value had come to be seen as a toxic mix of soaring short-term corporate profits, astronomic executive pay, along with stagnant median incomes, growing inequality, periodic massive financial crashes, declining corporate life expectancy, slowing productivity, declining rates of return on assets and overall, a widening distrust in business.

---

[127] See note 8.
[128] S. Pearlstein, "Top CEOs are Reclaiming Legitimacy by Advancing a Vision of What's Good for America," *The Washington Post*, August 19, 2019, www.washingtonpost.com/business/2019/08/19/top-ceos-are-reclaiming-legitimacy-by-advancing-vision-whats-good-america/.

7.2.2 Ditching "the World's Dumbest Idea"

Now the BRT has recognized that a sole focus on profits for shareholders is no longer defensible and has redefined business purpose. As Pearlstein explains:

> "In the Roundtable's new formulation of corporate purpose, delivering value to customers, investing in employees, dealing fairly and honestly with suppliers, supporting communities and protecting the environment all have equal billing with generating long-term value for shareholders. The statement rejects the idea of 'maximizing' one value to the exclusion of all the others. Instead, it acknowledges the need for balance and compromise in serving all the firm's stakeholders."

It's good news that major corporations have recognized that a sole focus on shareholders is financially, socially, and economically wrong.

7.2.3 Loss of Clarity

It's less good news that the purpose of a firm is now even murkier. The BRT statement seems to be less a clarification of corporate purpose and more a defensive reaction to the complaints about big business.

We will thus soon be hearing many more preachy corporate purpose statements with a capital "P," that sound good but have little or no actionable content. From outside the corporation, it may be even more difficult to figure out what goals firms are really pursuing.

Even inside the corporation, when managers are doing their utmost to show that they are "not maximizing one value to the exclusion of all others," there is a risk that managers themselves may become unclear in their own minds which priorities they should be pursuing. In effect, if corporations start seriously pursuing multiple-stakeholder value, with no stakeholder having priority over any other, the managers themselves may lose track of which direction they are heading.

8 The Mirage of Stakeholder Capitalism

8.1 Why Stakeholder Capitalism Will Fail

This section examines the widely cited narrative – embraced in 2019 by the BRT – that the purpose of a corporation should be to add value to all the stakeholders. The first snapshot shows why stakeholder capitalism is likely to fail for the same reasons that it failed in the mid-20th century: it fails to set direction and encourages the emergence of rudderless companies. The article was first published in Forbes.com on January 5, 2020[129]

"We should seize this moment," wrote Klaus Schwab, Founder and Executive Chairman, World Economic Forum, "to ensure that stakeholder capitalism remains the new dominant model."

Indeed, stakeholder capitalism – the notion that a firm focuses on meeting the needs of all its stakeholders – is now on almost every top executive's lips. After decades of declaring fealty to the goal of maximizing shareholder value, big business now admits that maximizing shareholder value is wrong and claims to be aiming at creating value for all the stakeholders.

The support for stakeholder capitalism comes as we enter a new decade and big business finds itself under attack from all sides: it has been caught single-mindedly shoveling money to its shareholders and its executives at the expense of customers, employees, the environment, and society. Now it declares it support of all the stakeholders. Will this new gambit work?

8.1.1 Stakeholder Capitalism

Stakeholder capitalism is now everywhere. It's the theme of the Davos Manifesto 2020, and the mantra of the BRT since 2019. Yet if big business were to implement stakeholder capitalism, it seems likely to fail for the same reason that it failed in the twentieth century. Its fatal flaw was that it offers no guidance as to what "true North" for a corporation is.

When big firms attempted to implement it for several decades in the mid-twentieth century, the perpetual need throughout the organization to keep balancing conflicting claims among stakeholders led not only to mass confusion. It eventually provoked a resort to maximizing shareholder value, the very thing for which big business is now being assailed.

---

[129] S. Denning, "Why Stakeholder Capitalism Will Fail," *Forbes.com*, January 5, 2020, www.forbes.com/sites/stevedenning/2020/01/05/why-stakeholder-capitalism-will-fail/.

8.1.2 Stakeholder Capitalism as a PR Front

What's going on here? Informed critics have concluded that stakeholder capitalism in most firms is nothing more than an elaborate public relations stunt espoused by big business to get through the current PR crisis. Business, they say, will go on doing what it has done since time immemorial: making money for itself.

The attraction of stakeholder capitalism as a public stance is that it doesn't commit big business to do anything in particular. Firms can go on privately shoveling money to their shareholders and executives, while maintaining a façade of exquisite social sensitivity and exemplary altruism.

There is of course a grain of truth in stakeholder capitalism. Big business must ultimately pay attention to all its stakeholders, including shareholders. When big business shortchanges stakeholders other than shareholders and executives, the stock market might soar in the short term but the decades-long diversion of business income in public companies to shareholders has resulted in stagnating incomes for most of the population. As inequality increased, populist leaders emerged with the risk that the political consensus holding countries together could unravel.

8.1.3 The True North of a Corporation: Value for Customers

In announcing the Davos Manifesto 2020, the chair of the World Economic Forum, Klaus Schwab argued that there were only three alternatives: shareholder capitalism, state capitalism, and stakeholder capitalism. Both shareholder capitalism and state capitalism were now both political poison. So, Schwab argued, the only alternative was stakeholder capitalism. QED.

In opting for stakeholder capitalism, Schwab missed a better option: customer capitalism. The most successful firms today are those that pursue what Peter Drucker long ago saw to be "true North" for a corporation: creating customers. Generating fresh value for customers is the foundation for generating benefits for all the stakeholders. Drucker saw that there were many other things firms also needed to take care of, but the overriding goal – which all the forces of a firm must support for the firm to survive – is to create customers.

8.1.4 The Origin – and Return – of Stakeholder Capitalism

As the critique of big business entered the political sphere, the notion that firms are "serving the needs of all the stakeholders" has come to be seen as a safe haven for firms under attack.

What the idea overlooks is that big firms comprise coalitions of participants and groupings whose goals often conflict. "Stakeholder capitalism" with its call to balance the claims of different stakeholders in every decision could have made some sense for major issues at the level of the C-suite, for instance, when a decision on a huge investment is at stake.

But when it is applied to decision-making throughout the firm, it throws innumerable decisions into a morass of differing viewpoints, values, attitudes, and ambitions, to be made by different people at different levels of the organization.

8.1.5 The Emergence of Dilbert-Style Managers

Inside the corporation, in the absence of clear preferences or guidelines among stakeholders, managers themselves can become unclear in their own minds which priorities they should be pursuing. One result is the Dilbert-style manager.

The skill set and the attitudes of the Dilbert-style manager were identified in a famous *Harvard Business Review* article in 1977: Abraham Zaleznik's "Managers and Leaders: Are They Different?" *HBR* has republished the article multiple times.[130]

In the article, Zaleznik deftly describes the practices and attitudes of the Dilbertian manager.

- **First, the manager focuses attention on procedure and not on substance.** The manager focuses attention on *how* the decisions are made, not *what* decisions to make. That's because the manager is typically working in a bureaucratic setting where the goals of the organization are neither clear nor perceived as worthwhile. In the place of goals that provide meaning at work and in work, there is a hierarchical structure, precise role definitions, and elaborate rules and procedures, which often conflict: managers have no way of knowing what the right answer is. The only safe place is to focus on process.
- **Second, the manager communicates to subordinates indirectly by signals**, rather than clearly stating a position. The traditional rule-driven bureaucracy requires both managers and workers to leave their personal views and attitudes behind, before they enter the workplace. In this world, the managers' personal views are irrelevant. The only safe way to communicate is to make use of the rules and deploy indirect "signals," which obscure who

---

[130] A. Zaleznik, "Managers and Leaders: Are They Different?" *Harvard Business Review*, 1977, 82 (1), pp. 74–81, https://hbr.org/2004/01/managers-and-leaders-are-they-different; S. Denning, "A dangerous thought? Do managers need to be leaders?," October 7, 2010, http://stevedenning.typepad.com/steve_denning/2010/07/a-dangerous-thought-do-managers-need-to-be-leaders.html.

wins and who loses. The manager can hide behind process: "It is not what I believe that matters: It is what the system requires."

- **Third, the manager plays for time**. With conflicting rules and procedures, and conflicts about priorities between different senior managers, mid-level managers have no way of knowing what the right answer is. The idea of using their own judgment is at odds with the idea that they left their own views behind. Hence playing for time and waiting for the dust to settle are ways of always being on the winning side. These CYA routines are played out, up and down the hierarchy.

These Dilbertian practices enable a mid-level manager to survive. They have also helped cartoonist Scott Adams make a fortune depicting how these practices played out on a daily basis in firms around the world,

The further result is the disparagement of the discipline of management itself, with calls for "leaders, not managers." The problem is not so much managers, but rather the concept of management that firms impose. When top management fails to set direction, how can managers at lower levels accomplish that?

8.2 The Second Dumbest Idea in The World: Firms with Preachy Social Purposes

The second snapshot in this section suggests that if shareholder value is the dumbest idea in the world, then stakeholder capitalism may be the world's second dumbest. It shows that preachy social purposes are often deployed implausibly to communicate goals that the firms don't systematically pursue, such as Mars Inc.'s efforts to use a positive environmental goal of protecting the world's forests as topping for its chocolate business.[131] The article was first published in Forbes.com on October 27, 2019.[132]

It's easy to see why big business is in disrepute. Whether it's the oil companies' systematic promotion of fossil fuels at the expense of climate change, big tech playing fast and loose with our privacy and our democracy, large pharma growing rich from selling high-priced drugs, manufacturers transferring whole industries along with their jobs to China or Mexico, big banks creating a mammoth financial crisis without being held accountable, executives' self-dealing through share buybacks and exorbitant compensation, or the growing concentration of market power in many sectors, it's no wonder that Americans' once-sunny view of big business has shifted towards disapproval.

---

[131] S. Denning, "Second Dumbest Idea: Firms with Preachy Social Purposes," *Forbes.com*, October 27, 2019, www.forbes.com/sites/stevedenning/2019/10/27/the-second-dumbest-idea-in-the-world-firms-with-preachy-social-purposes/.
[132] Ibid.

While in 1950 a poll found that 60% of Americans had a favorable opinion of large firms, by 2017, that number had declined to 21% in a Gallup poll.[133] Today, politician after politician promises remedial or even punitive action, and in August, big business itself signaled a shift: the Business Roundtable, the influential US business group, renounced its two-decades-old declaration that "corporations exist principally to serve their shareholders," yet without really clarifying what businesses *do* exist for.

Some reformers cry that firms must put "purpose before profit" and declare lofty social purposes. Take for instance the recent series of articles in the *Financial Times* on the theme of "purpose and profit." It illustrates how the addition of wider social purposes risks delivering us from greed at the cost of corporate confusion. In the articles, Royal Dutch Shell, Novo Nordisk, Hitachi, Levi Strauss, Mars Inc., and Danone are cited as exemplars of firms that are trying to "combine profit with purpose."

Yet while it's welcome that maximizing shareholder value is increasingly being recognized as – in the words of Jack Welch – "the world's dumbest idea" – imagining that corporations might get out of their self-constructed moral doghouse by grafting a preachy social purpose on top of their profit motive may well be the world's second dumbest idea.

8.2.1 Why Preachy Social Purposes Don't Cut It

After several decades in which maximizing shareholder value has been the corporate orthodoxy, shareholder value is now embedded in the mindset, habits, practices, processes, and systems of big business. It is enforced by Wall Street and its preoccupation with short-term profits, at least in the case of firms that have no clear long-term growth strategy. Merely declaring a "wider social purpose" on top of these existing mindsets, processes, and systems is unlikely to create more than a façade behind which corporations will continue operating as before.

Indeed, the group of companies that *Financial Times* has assembled to illustrate the "firm with a broader social purpose" illustrate the issue.

8.2.2 The Case of Mars Inc.

If Mars Inc. is to be the inspiration of "a firm with a wider purpose" as a result of its concern for nutrition, it would be good to know how this

---

[133] R. Atkinson, "Learning to Love Big Business," *The Atlantic*, April 2018, www.theatlantic.com /magazine/archive/2018/04/learning-to-love-big-business/554096/.

wider purpose relates to its actual business of making and selling products of such dubious nutritional value as Mars bars, Milky Way bars, M&M's, Skittles, Snickers, Twix, nonconfectionery snacks, Combos, and pet foods. It is one thing to talk about nutrition. It is another to be doing something meaningful about it.

The failure to make progress against deforestation has tarnished the image and credibility of the chocolate industry at a time when it is already under fire for its practices in West Africa. *The Washington Post* reported in June 2019 about the use of child labor in West African cocoa fields, which has persisted despite promises to stop it. Mars, Nestlé and Hershey pledged long ago to stop using cocoa harvested by children. Yet much of the chocolate you buy still starts with child labor.[134]

In 2019, Mars postponed its target date for switching entirely to sustainably produced cocoa from 2020 to 2025. "Zero deforestation cocoa only exists where all the forest has already disappeared," wrote Francois Ruf, an economist with CIRAD, a French agricultural research and international cooperation organization.

Traders, certification firms and the Ivorian and Ghanaian governments are struggling alongside chocolate companies to find a strategy that works. Mars, for example, has paid tens of millions of dollars extra for certified cocoa, and millions more to certification firms such as Rainforest Alliance. Now, however, it is skeptical that it can deliver, given the difficulty of monitoring the thousands of cocoa farmers scratching out harvests on small plots.

The sad truth is that we have been down the path of purpose diversification before, with disastrous results. There is no point in going there again.

8.3 Why the Pandemic of Maximizing Shareholder Value Is Still Raging

The third snapshot in this section shows why the pandemic of maximizing share-holder value is still raging and continues to be the main operating model for most large public firms, with the same disastrous effects that it had over the last half-century. The article was published in Forbes.com on March 21, 2022.[135]

---

[134] S. Mufson, "The Trouble with Chocolate," *The Washington Post*, October 29, 2019, www .washingtonpost.com/graphics/2019/national/climate-environment/mars-chocolate-deforest ation-climate-change-west-africa/.

[135] S. Denning, "Why MSV Is Still Dominant," *Forbes.com*, March 21, 2022, www.forbes.com/ sites/stevedenning/2022/03/21/why-the-pandemic-of-maximizing-shareholder-value-is-still-dominant/.

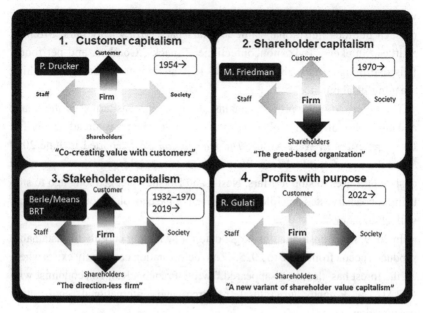

Figure 26 Four main types of corporate purpose

Despite capitalism's two-century track record of improving most people's lives on every major material indicator, capitalism now faces a crisis of legitimacy. "A movement to reset capitalism is already underway," the *Financial Times* says. "Lots of business-people are now talking about purpose and the need to instill new ways beyond pure shareholder value." The question is whether the new ways will make things better or worse.

8.3.1 Prior Missteps on Corporate Purpose

The last ninety years have seen several missteps on corporate purpose. The narrative of stakeholder capitalism was launched in 1932, by Adolf Berle and Gardiner Means in their book, *The Modern Corporation and Private Property.* From the 1930s onward, corporate managers embraced "stakeholder capitalism" (Figure 26(3)). Managers were expected to optimize among all the stakeholders – customers, staff and partners, shareholders, and society as a whole. The result when this approach was adopted for decision-making throughout the firm was indecision and confusion.

In September 1970, Nobel-Prize winning economist Milton Friedman's famous *New York Times* article, followed by the efforts of his collaborators, economics professors Michael Jensen and William Meckling, conceived and launched the virus of maximizing shareholder value on an unsuspecting world (see Figure 26(2)).

Fifty years later, the resulting maximizing shareholder value pandemic is still raging with well-documented, disastrous consequences: short-termism, distrust, income and wealth inequality, declining financial returns and lower long-term shareholder value.

It wasn't capitalism itself that caused all these problems: it was the virus of maximizing shareholder value as reflected? in the current stock price that is still going strong.

8.3.2 Why the Shareholder Value Virus Still Lives On

In August 2019, hundreds of CEOs of big firms in the BRT formally renounced their support of maximizing shareholder value. Yet the renunciation was as effective against the shareholder value pandemic as a porous facemask is against COVID-19. Maximizing shareholder value is still embedded in most big firms' goals, strategies, plans, processes, budgets, sales, and marketing processes – basically everything – as shown in Figure 16.

And it's not just *inside* the firms. The continuing impact of the shareholder value pandemic is reflected in below-average financial results, of firms like IBM, GE, Electrolux, and many others. Even if we get to a point when firms truly accept that maximizing shareholder value is a noxious idea, it will still take years to undo the damage done by the MSV virus to firms and to society.

Thus, the BRT declaration of 2019 didn't kill the maximizing shareholder value virus. On the surface, it merely returned us to the confusion of the very stakeholder capitalism that had failed us in the mid-twentieth century (Figure 26(3)).

In theory, managers are now supposed to optimize among the stakeholders – customers, staff and partners, shareholders, and staff in the interests of society. "But if all stakeholders are essential," says Wharton School finance professor, Raghuram G. Rajan, "then none are."[136] Not surprisingly, since maximizing shareholder value is by now entrenched in most firms' processes, these firms have continued as before, that is, with maximizing shareholder value. Is this a surprise when executives are richly compensated for doing so?

8.3.3 Yet Another Misstep: "Profit and Purpose"

Now, as the emptiness in the BRT 2019 declaration has been documented, a new effort is under way by some members of the commentariat to set matters right by

---

[136] R. G. Rajan, "What Should Corporations Do?" *Project Syndicate*, October 6, 2020, www .project-syndicate.org/commentary/what-are-corporations-for-stakeholders-or-shareholders-by-raghuram-rajan-2020-10.

proposing that firms travel in two different directions at the same time, as shown in Figure 26(4): "profits with purpose."

Going in two different directions at the same time may seem less confusing than going in four different directions at the same time as in stakeholder value in Figure 26(3), but, in substance, the error is the same: you can only go in one direction at once.

The *Financial Times* wrote in 2019 that big companies, by signing the BRT declaration, had "turned cuddly."[137] It wasn't so. It turned out that the Business Roundtable renunciation of shareholder value was not for real.

Real-world solutions are not about becoming cuddly. They are about becoming more tough minded about what works and what doesn't. Inequality today is mainly generated by the lethal virus of MSV that was concocted in the laboratory of Milton Friedman and his collaborators in 1970s. Hard tough-mindedness and firm action are needed to rid us of this virus, along with the inequality and short-termism that it spawned.

---

[137] J. Sinclair, "Is 2019 the Year Companies Turned Cuddly?" *Financial Times*, December 20, 2019, www.ft.com/video/0865add9-03c1-4623-a249-ac2d71abcdd4.

9 Conclusions and Reflections

This Element has examined three over-arching management narratives: customer capitalism, shareholder capitalism, and stakeholder capitalism, and their role in the emerging digital age.

Capitalism's future is inherently uncertain, unpredictable, and complex. Moreover, capitalism itself is a embedded in even wider systems affected by events that include the ongoing war in Europe, a COVID-19 pandemic that continues to rage, increasing inflation and economic slowdowns, extreme politicization amid struggles between democracy and autocracy, uncertain twists and turns in global politics, and the risks of major climate change. Amid such uncertainties, we can at best gather and evaluate information, explore hypotheses and assess probabilities.

Subject to these caveats, eight conclusions follow.

9.1 Capitalism Should Not Be Scrapped

First, given capitalism's track record, it should not be scrapped. Despite many flaws, capitalism has brought vast material benefits to the human race over several centuries. There is no reason to believe that the means of production and their operation for profit should be transferred from the private, to the public, sector. Instead, effort should be directed to understanding capitalism's flaws and taking steps to remedy them and adapt capitalism to a rapidly changing world.

At the same time, the relative strengths of the public and private sectors should be kept steadily in mind so that appropriate adjustments at the margin can be made. For instance, in dealing with the COVID-19 pandemic in 2020, bold steps by various governments to make direct public sector investments to accelerate private sector development of vaccines helped avert an even greater calamity that would have occurred if action had been left entirely to the private sector. The result was the production of remarkably effective vaccines extraordinarily rapidly, even though the global distribution of vaccines that were developed was less than equitable.[138]

9.2 Recognize and Accept the Birth of a New Age

Second, understanding the role of capitalism must reflect a wider recognition that we are experiencing the predictable birth pangs of a new economic age – the digital age. As the industrial era becomes steadily less central, we are entering a period that is upending workplaces and corporations, and destabilizing parts

---

[138] J. Feinmann, "Covid-19: Global Vaccine Production is a Mess and Shortages are Down to More Than Just Hoarding," *BMJ*, October 28, 2021, www.bmj.com/content/375/bmj.n2375.

of our economy and our political systems. It is challenging power relationships, as well as the privileges and prerogatives of elites, and creating a new battlefield on which the power struggles of today are being fought.[139]

Yet the benefits of the new age are extraordinary and irresistible. When offered the possibility of making our lives cheaper, easier, more convenient, speedier, more agreeable, and more relevant to our needs, with greater capabilities than the richest king or emperor in history, we as customers and users have chosen. There is no going back. We are already in a new age, though still finding our way.

Most industrial-era firms are still making money, but they can also see even greater riches being heaped on the digital winners. As a result, they too are pouring money into digital initiatives and Agile transformations. Yet without deeper change from industrial-era mindsets towards democratized leadership, they are often frustrated when their investments do not generate the intended benefit.[140]

The transition to the digital age is inexorable. The main question now is whether it will be accomplished quickly and fairly, with the benefits shared widely, and responsively to the needs of the environment, or whether it will be driven by the same greed and thoughtlessness that drove the aberrant share-holder-value capitalism of the last half-century.

9.3 Firms Should Commit to Customer Capitalism

A third conclusion is that the best fit with the digital age is customer capitalism, which gives primacy to co-creating value for customers, while not ignoring other stakeholders. This is not surprising because customer capitalism took off in response to the problems of managing software in a bureaucracy. When firms embrace the new, more agile ways of creating value for customers, they can shift direction more nimbly, create great workplaces, get better talent and use it more effectively, win over customers more quickly, attract more finance, do their share in meeting social and environmental goals more readily, and generate more long-term shareholder value.

The core idea of customer capitalism is simple to understand. Love your customer as yourself. This is not only ethical. It is also very effective. People do best when what they do is in the service of delighting others. When they are able

---

[139] A. Toffler, *The Third Wave* (Random House, 1984), p. 10.

[140] S. Denning, "Why Digital Transformations Are Failing," *Forbes.com*, May 23, 2021, www .forbes.com/sites/stevedenning/2021/05/23/why-digital-transformations-are-failing/;
S. Denning, "What JPMorgan Must Do to Get the Stock Market's Respect," *Forbes.com*, May 30, 2022, www.forbes.com/sites/stevedenning/2022/05/30/what-jpmorgan-must-do-to-get-the-stock-markets-respect/.

to work on something worthwhile with others who love doing the same thing, the group tends to get better. By working in short cycles, everyone can see the outcome of what is being done. When communications are interactive and everyone is open about what is going on, problems get solved. Innovation can occur. Customers are surprised to find that even unexpressed desires are being met. Work can become fun.

The goal of giving primacy to customers is gaining traction among leading firms. For instance, a review shows that eighteen of the thirty leading firms in the Dow Jones Industrial Index have already committed to customer primacy in their mission statements. Of these eighteen firms, eleven are performing better in terms of total return over five years than the average of S&P 500 firms.[141]

The fact that seven of the eighteen firms that have mission statements committed to customer primacy are performing below the average S&P 500, confirms that merely declaring a mission is by itself not enough to achieve a higher level of performance: firms have to actually implement the mission.

9.4 Include the "Why," the "How," and the "What" of Customer Capitalism

A fourth conclusion is that for firms to succeed in customer capitalism, they must tackle the "why" and the "how" of the firm's behavior, not just the "what."

9.4.1 Start with Getting the "Why" Right

Customer capitalism is about human beings co-creating value for other human beings. Different firms have different formulations of the same core idea. Including, "zero distance to customers;" and "the experience economy."

Staff working in self-organizing teams can have a direct line of sight to the customers who use the firm's products and services. This way of working is not only effective. It feels right. Firms pursuing customer primacy, such as Amazon, Apple, and Microsoft, have become the most valuable firms on the planet. They got the "why" of business right.

9.4.2 Don't Forget the "How"

Yet getting the "why" right is not enough. Firms also need to execute on the "how." In order to create people-centered organizations, organizations need people-centered processes. They need systems that keep the organization focused on systematically achieving people-relevant outcomes, rather than

---

[141] S. Denning, "Why Your Mission Statement Must Include Customer Primacy," *Forbes.com*, May 22, 2022, www.forbes.com/sites/stevedenning/2022/05/22/why-your-mission-statement-must-include-customer-primacy/.

merely the production of outputs. They need processes that continually push the organization to delight and enchant their customers routinely and signal when this is not happening. They need arrangements that enable the organization to draw on the full talents and creativity of the people doing the work.

Today's winning firms are far from perfect. Amazon got the "why" of business right, but has made mistakes in the "how." As Jean-Louis Barsoux and colleagues write in *Harvard Business Review*: "Take Amazon. In its determination to be 'customer obsessed,' it was blind to the needs of another constituency: its merchants. It squeezed them on fees, forced them to compete with other vendors and its own knockoffs, restricted their ability to customize virtual storefronts, and limited their access to payment options."[142] Similarly, many of Amazon's lower level workplaces, including some fulfilment centers, do not reflect the creative aspects of its higher level workplaces.

Or take Verizon, a firm with a strong commitment to customer primacy in its mission statement. Anecdotal evidence suggests that the mission statement is not yet fully implemented in practice, as Columbia University business strategy professor, Rita McGrath, explains the customer realities of dealing with Verizon.[143]

9.4.3 Don't Get Lost In the "What"

The greed implicit in maximizing shareholder value constitutes both a performance, and an ethical, problem. But pleading with managers to establish cultures of psychological safety, set up ethics committees, have training classes in ethics, or appoint managers with more character and integrity, all risk getting lost in the "what" of the firm's behavior.[144] Unless firms get the "why" and the "how," reforms at the level of the "what" will be ineffective. Firms must align all three.

9.5 Firms Should Terminate Shareholder Capitalism

Fifth, maximizing shareholder value should be ended as soon as possible. This form of capitalism maximizes benefits for shareholders and executives at the expense of all other stakeholders and society. It destroys long-term shareholder value, instills short-termism, and leads to astronomic executive pay, stagnant

---

[142] J.-L. Barsoux, M. Wade, and C. Bouquet, "Identifying Unmet Needs in a Digital Age," *Harvard Business Review*, July 2022, https://hbr.org/2022/07/identifying-unmet-needs-in-a-digital-age.

[143] R. McGrath, "The Better Your Automated Customer Service Options, the Worse Your Customer Service Experience," *Rita McGrath Group*, April 7, 2021, www.ritamcgrath.com/sparks/2021/04/the-better-your-automated-customer-service-options-the-worse-your-customer-service-experience/.

[144] S. Denning, "How to Reconcile Management and Morality in Today's Gilded Age," *Forbes.com*, June 22, 2022, www.forbes.com/sites/stevedenning/2022/06/22/how-to-reconcile-management-and-morality-in-todays-gilded-age/.

median incomes, growing inequality, increasing financialization, periodic financial crashes, declining corporate life expectancy, and overall, a widening distrust in business.

Shareholder capitalism was renounced by the Business Roundtable in 2019, and is now mostly implemented behind a PR façade of stakeholder capitalism.

In part, that's because change is hard. The management principles and processes that follow from shareholder value – bureaucracy, hierarchy, autocratic leadership, backward looking strategy, sales and marketing focused on short-term profit, and control-oriented HR – are still embedded in most large firms. Even if firms want to change, corporations run in this fashion cannot adapt rapidly. Changing all those practices, procedures, policies, and attitudes, will be a major undertaking.

In part, it's because, even if firms practicing shareholder capitalism want to contribute significantly to social and environmental goals, or pay their workers more fairly, they often lack the financial means to do so. As they are held on a tight leash by the stock market and treated as cash cows to fund more promising growth stocks, their principal challenge is often just to survive from quarter to quarter.

In part, it's because executives and investors still believe in it. It has been a major part of executives' careers and key to attaining the executive positions they now hold. In the short-term, shareholder capitalism can be seen as a success because it generates gains for shareholders and the executives themselves.

In effect, although in the long run, this aberration of capitalism is doomed, its removal is not going to be simple or quick.

9.6 Don't Get Lost in Stakeholder Capitalism

Sixth, firms should not get lost in the most widely cited form of capitalism today: stakeholder capitalism. Since 2019, this goal has been promoted by both businesses and their critics, albeit with different meanings. It is mostly used by firms as a façade to enable them to maintain the status quo and pursue shareholder capitalism.

The label of stakeholder capitalism gives firms the breathing space to get on with logging short-term profits, meeting their expected quarterly returns, and snagging their growing bonuses. Beneath the protestations of public good, actions often remain self-serving.

Ironically, would-be reformers of capitalism also champion stakeholder capitalism They tend to view it as an improvement over shareholder capitalism, but often fail to see that it is incoherent as a practical guide to action for an entire firm. It is no more real than the holy grail, and the pursuit of it is likely to be equally futile.

9.7 Governments Must Play a More Active Role

Seventh, governments must play a more active role in some areas. The aberrant form of capitalism of the last half century is like a virus ravaging the economy. It is perhaps the last desperation move by industrial firms economy to preserve themselves before they succumb to the digital age.

The greater understanding that we now have of the different phases of the life cycle of capitalism, shows how government might help dismantling shareholder capitalism by removing the various ways in which the public sector supports it. The specific steps will depend on each individual country.

The following are priorities that the United States should address:

- Reexamine SEC regulations that facilitate the extraction of wealth from corporations, despite obvious conflicts of interest and self-dealing by executives.[145]
- Reexamine the tax laws so that large firms are required to pay a fair share of taxes, along with an international treaty on minimum taxes on multinationals.
- Reexamine the legal arrangements that permit seemingly unreasonable non-compete agreements for some forty million workers.[146]

Some of these changes are currently under consideration.

9.8 Recognize the Length of the Journey to Customer Capitalism

Finally, firms should prepare themselves for the journey from industrial-era capitalism to customer capitalism. As digital winners shower benefits on customers and users, and the stock market lavishes gains on the digital winners, most executives can see the need for change.

As they realize that the organization must up its own game to cope with the fast-changing marketplace, the move for change increasingly comes from the top. In effect, the question shifts from "Why do we have to change?" to: "Why can't we have what they're having?"

Top managers increasingly realize that success not only needs a fundamentally different way of managing, leading, and thinking: they are starting to see that they too will have to change.[147] Within many large

---

[145] Ö. Tulum, A. Andreoni, and W. Lazonick, *Financialisation to Innovation in UK Big Pharma* (Cambridge University Press, forthcoming).

[146] www.whitehouse.gov/briefing-room/statements-releases/2021/07/09/fact-sheet-executive-order-on-promoting-competition-in-the-american-economy/.

[147] A study by the executive search firm, Egon Zehnder, suggests that "83% leaders find it essential to reflect on their own leadership style": https://hr.economictimes.indiatimes.com/news/trends/78-of-ceos-agree-to-continue-their-self-transformation-as-hybrid-work-continues-study/86288315.

organizations, fruitful discussions are occurring. There are often significant islands of change advocates. For some, the shift is non-negotiable. If the firm won't support change, the best talent goes elsewhere.

There is increasing recognition that the new way of running organizations is more than a set of tools. It's about conveying meaning that reveals our deepest values, our very core, as human beings. It entails a different state of mind that starts with a change of heart.

The discussions within firms tend to proceed slowly, as this is not just about changing a single tool. It's a massive rethinking and reimagining of many traditional principles of management, as shown in Figure 16 in Section 4. The changes cut deep.

Anecdotal evidence suggests that leaders who are succeeding in these discussions are discovering that it gives them the chance to live and lead with satisfaction and even joy in their work. They think and feel differently about their organization and their lives.

Thus, the new way of getting things done is a transformative idea. Like all transformative ideas, it creates an intellectual frame by which other ideas can be evaluated. It offers a way out of many practical, financial, economic, social, political, and ethical dilemmas of our time. It establishes criteria by which goals can be set and progress measured. Instead of offering a jigsaw puzzle of little fixes, it provides a broad theory of how organizations – and society – can function for the better.

As support for the new way of doing things becomes more widespread, debates will continue about the details of implementation, of emphasis, of terminology, and so on. Entrenched opposition will have to be overcome. Improved practices will be discovered. More sophisticated measures will emerge. Wrong turnings will have to be recognized as such. Some practices will be discarded. But there is no need to wait for course corrections in order to move forward. The direction ahead is clear.

That's because the different way of doing things can generate a prospect that is genuinely exciting. It can clarify the present and point to a better future. It is a practical path towards a world that is better for those doing the work, better for those for whom the work is being done, better for the organizations that coordinate the work and better for society,

Two subsequent Elements in this series on Reinventing Capitalism will deepen the discussion begun in this Element. One will examine in detail the steps in the journey flagged in Section 4. The other will expand the analysis of historical and multicountry perspectives of shareholder capitalism outlined in Section 7.

Select Bibliography

Andreessen, M. "Why Software Is Eating the World." *Wall Street Journal*, August 20, 2011

Atkinson, R. "Learning to Love Big Business." *The Atlantic*, April 2018

Backhouse, R. E. and Medema, S. "Retrospectives: On the Definition of Economics." *Journal of Economic Perspectives*. Winter 2009, 23(1), pp. 221–233

Bebchuk, L. and Tallarita, R. "'Stakeholder' Capitalism Seems Mostly for Show." *Wall Street Journal*, August 6, 2020

Benoit, D. "Move Over, Shareholders: Top CEOs Say Companies Have Obligations to Society." *Wall Street Journal*, August 19, 2019

Bivens, J. and Mishel, L. "Understanding the Historic Divergence between Productivity and a Typical Worker." *Economic Policy Institute*, Report, September 2, 2015

Blankenship, B. "Why the Stock Market Is Not the Real Economy." *CGTN*, October 13, 2020.

Brettell, K., Gaffen, D. and Rohde, D. "The Cannibalized Company: How the Cult of Shareholder Value Has Reshaped Corporate America; A Special Report." *Reuters*, November 16, 2015

Chainey, R. "Beyond GDP: Time to Rethink How We Measure Growth." *World Economic Forum*, June 4, 2016.

Dalio, R. *Changing World Order: Why Nations Succeed and Fail.* Simon & Schuster, 2021, p. 31

Dayen, D. "Big Tech: The New Predatory Capitalism." *American Prospect*, Winter 2018

Denning, S. *The Leader's Guide to Radical Management.* Jossey-Bass, 2010

Denning, S. *The Leader's Guide to Storytelling*, 2nd ed. Jossey-Bass, 2011

Denning, S. *The Age of Agile.* HarperCollins, 2018

Drucker, P. *The Practice of Management.* Harper and Brothers, 1954

Forbes. "Top 33 Companies for the Environment." *Forbes.com*, April 22, 2019

Fowler, G. "Big Tech CEO Hearing Lies." *The Washington Post*, July 29, 2020

Gelles, D. and Yaffe-Bellany, D. "Shareholder Value Is No Longer Everything, Top C.E.O.s Say." *The New York Times*, August 19, 2019

Guerra, F. "Welch Condemns Share Price Focus." *Financial Times*, March 12, 2009

Harvey, D. *Seventeen Contradictions and the End of Capitalism.* Oxford University Press, 2014

Hastings, H. "The New Economics of Value and Value Creation." *Economics for Business*, March 29, 2021.

Henderson, R. "US Companies Cling to Share Buybacks Despite Collapse in Profits." *Financial Times*, July 30, 2020

Henderson, R. and Temple, P. "Group of US Corporate Leaders Ditches Shareholder-First Mantra." *Financial Times*, August 19, 2019

Horsley, S. "After 2 Years, Trump Tax Cuts Have Failed to Deliver on GOP's Promises." *NPR*, December 20, 2019

Iansiti, M. and Nadella, S. "Democratizing Transformation." *Harvard Business Review*, May–June 2022

Jensen, M. "CEO Incentives: Not How Much but How." *Harvard Business Review*, May 1990

Khanna, R. *Dignity in the Digital Age*. Simon & Schuster, 2022

Kolhatkar, S. "Lina Khan & Big Tech." *New Yorker*, December 12, 2021

Krugman, P. and Wells, R. *Economics*, 3rd ed. Worth, 2012, p. 2

Lazonick, W. "Profits without Prosperity." *Harvard Business Review*, September 2014

Martin, R. "The Age of Customer Capitalism." *Harvard Business Review*, January 2010

Martin, R. *Fixing the Game: Bubbles, Crashes, and What Capitalism Can Learn from the NFL*. HBRP, 2011

Mufson, S. "The Trouble with Chocolate." *The Washington Post*, October 29, 2019

Murray, A. "Profits and Purpose: Can Big Business Have It Both Ways?" *Fortune*, August 19, 2019

Nair, L. Dalton, N. Hull, P. and Kerr, W. "Use Purpose to Transform Your Workplace." *Harvard Business Review*, March 2022

Oremus, W. "How Bezos Went Thermonuclear on Diapers." *Slate*, October 2013

Overton, M. *Agricultural Revolution in England: The Transformation of the Agrarian Economy 1500-1850*. Cambridge University Press, 1996.

Pérez, C. *Technological Revolutions and Financial Capital: The Dynamics of Bubbles and Golden Ages*. Edward Elgar, 2003

Plender, J. "Blowing the Whistle on Buybacks and Value Destruction." *Financial Times*, March 1, 2016

Rajan, R. G. "What Should Corporations Do?" *Project Syndicate*, October 6, 2020

Rigby, D., Elk, S., and Berez, S. "Purposeful Business the Agile Way." *Harvard Business Review*, March 2022

Savitz, E. J. "Big Tech Is in a Perilous Moment." *Barron's*, August 20, 2021

Schumpeter, J. A. *Capitalism, Socialism and Democracy*. Routledge, 1994 [1942]

Shiller, R. *Narrative Economics: How Stories Go Viral and Drive Major Economic Events*. Princeton University Press, 2019

Sinclair, J. "Is 2019 the Year Companies Turned Cuddly?" *Financial Times*, December 20, 2019

Solow, R. "We'd Better Watch Out." *The New York Times*, July 12, 1987

Steiber, A. *Management in the Digital Age: Will China Surpass Silicon Valley?* Springer, 2017

Steiber, A. *Leadership for a Digital World: The Transformation of GE Appliances*. Springer, 2022

Toffler, A. *The Third Wave*. Random House, 1984

Unseem, J. "Beware of Corporate Promises." *The Atlantic*, August 6, 2020

Wartzman, R. *The End of Loyalty: The Rise and Fall of Good Jobs in America*. Public Affairs, 2017

Will, G. F. "Man of the Century." *Hoover Digest*, October 30, 2002.

Zaleznik, A. "Managers and Leaders: Are They Different?" *Harvard Business Review*. 1977, 82(1), pp. 74–81

Cambridge Elements ⚌

Reinventing Capitalism

Arie Y. Lewin
Duke University

Arie Y. Lewin is Professor Emeritus of Strategy and International Business at Duke University, Fuqua School of Business. He is an Elected Fellow of the Academy of International Business and a Recipient of the Academy of Management inaugural Joanne Martin Trailblazer Award. Previously, he was Editor-in-Chief of *Management and Organization Review* (2015–2021) and the *Journal of International Business Studies* (2000–2007), founding Editor-in-Chief of *Organization Science* (1989–2007), and Convener of Organization Science Winter Conference (1990–2012). His research centers on studies of organizations' adaptation as co-evolutionary systems, the emergence of new organizational forms, and adaptive capabilities of innovating and imitating organizations. His current research focuses on de-globalization and decoupling, the Fourth Industrial Revolution, and the renewal of capitalism.

Till Talaulicar
University of Erfurt

Till Talaulicar holds the Chair of Organization and Management at the University of Erfurt where he is also the Dean of the Faculty of Economics, Law and Social Sciences. His main research expertise is in the areas of corporate governance and the responsibilities of the corporate sector in modern societies. Professor Talaulicar is Editor-in-Chief of *Corporate Governance: An International Review*, Senior Editor of *Management and Organization Review*, and serves on the Editorial Board of *Organization Science*. Moreover, he has been Founding Member and Chairperson of the Board of the International Corporate Governance Society (2014–2020).

Editorial Advisory Board

About the Series

This series seeks to feature explorations about the crisis of legitimacy facing capitalism today, including the increasing income and wealth gap, the decline of the middle class, threats to employment due to globalization and digitalization, undermined trust in institutions, discrimination against minorities, global poverty and pollution. Being grounded in a business and management perspective, the series incorporates contributions from multiple disciplines on the causes of the current crisis and potential solutions to renew capitalism.

Panmure House is the final and only remaining home of Adam Smith, Scottish philosopher and 'Father of modern economics.' Smith occupied the House between 1778 and 1790, during which time he completed the final editions of his master works: The Theory of Moral Sentiments and The Wealth of Nations. Other great luminaries and thinkers of the Scottish Enlightenment visited Smith regularly at the House across this period. Their mission is to provide a world-class twenty-first-century centre for social and economic debate and research, convening in the name of Adam Smith to effect positive change and forge global, future-focussed networks.

ADAM SMITH
PANMURE
HOUSE

Cambridge Elements ☰

Reinventing Capitalism

Printed in the United States
by Baker & Taylor Publisher Services